IN-HOUSE TEAM

Editor-in-chief: Caroline Blake

Sub-editor: Mike Toller

Designer: Anja Wohlstrom

Editorial & design assistant: Alexi Duggins

Production consultant: Iain Leslie

Cover design: James Cuddy and Jake Howard

Sales director: Brett MacDougall

National advertising manager: Sue Ostler

Web development: Cameron J Macphail

Accounts and HR: Sharon Evans

Operations director: Martin Dallaghan

Managing director: Ian Merricks

Publisher: IMD Group

Thanks to Katy Georgiou, Laura Jones and all previous contributors and photographers.

GLASGOW TEAM

City editor: Andrea Mullaney

Contributors: Amy Jenkins, Michael A. Fagan, Lisa Ann McQuillan, David Kirkwood, Iain Johnstone, Ann Russell, Lorna McKinnon, Joanna Bolouri, Lisa Melvin, Claire Snedden, Michelle Rosenberg, Joly Braime.

Photography: Angus Bremner, Shivy K, Roland Eva, Lloyd Bishop, Ibon San Martin, Matthew Bowden, Jorge Nassauer, Enver Uçarer , Mark Fletcher, Mirco Delcaldo Nathalie Dulex, Tim Ireland, Adam Elliston, Dave Tett.

Itchy Media Ltd
White Horse Yard
78 Liverpool Road
London
N1 0QD

Tel: 020 7288 9810
Fax: 020 7288 9815

E-mail: editor@itchymedia.co.uk
Web: www.itchycity.co.uk

ISBN: 1-905705-05-0, 978-1-905705-05-4

Welcome to Itchy 2006

We've trawled this green and pleasant land to bring you the finest guide to outing and abouting that our sceptred isle has to offer. We're bruised and battered after the escapades we've carried out in your honour, so the least you can do is follow our trail of destruction. Liver let die, eh? This book is bursting with cool bars, cosy pubs, lazy cafés and budget beds. We'll even tell you where to get hold of a slippery nipple at 4am. Team Itchy all have PhDs in misbehaviour; if it's debauchery you're after, we've got places to pull in and places to pass out in. The culture vultures are catered for too, from Caravaggio through to comedy. We've also done a spot of re–decorating since 2005, so we hope you like the new look. Bright and dynamic; a bit like your good selves. We've even given you shiny symbols to make your life that bit easier (have a gander below). Researched and written by locals, Itchy is your new best mate. Come on, let's get under the covers...

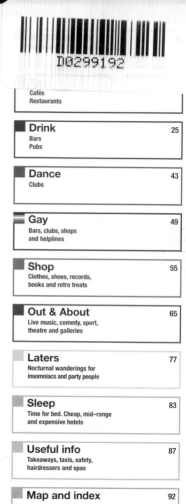

D0299192

- 🕐 Opening hours
- 🍴 Food
- 🍷 House wine
- 💷 Price

Introduction

Welcome to Glasgow

Ah, Glasgow. Home of the incomparable Billy Connolly, the unparalleled Charles Rennie Mackintosh and the suspiciously soupy-looking River Clyde.

So you've found yourself an Itchy guide. Great. Glasgow wants lucky devils like you. Whether you're sharp as a Scottish Claymore or squarer than David Coulthard's jaw, this city will suit you. You could be here for a day or for the rest of your life, but with a certain carefully researched little bible in your hip pocket, you'll find Glasgow has everything you need. Our little secret, eh?

Now we'd be lying if we claimed Glasgow's publicity over the years had all been as we'd have liked it, but as any Weegie in the know will tell you, the city offers more than just an opportunity to neck a bottle of 17-per-cent Buckfast and throw shopping trolleys in the Clyde. In recent years Glasgow has emerged from the shadows to scorn its critics and is now renowned for its smooth bars, salt-of-the-earth pubs and rocking clubs.

As you'd expect from a city with one of the most prestigious fine art schools in the country, Glasgow has art and design from the likes of the Burrell Collection, GOMA and the People's Palace, while the great designer and architect Charles Rennie Mackintosh has left his mark on the skyline for all to see. Glasgow has more theatres than any other UK city outside of London, its chefs are increasingly internationally renowned, and even its shopping centre has acquired an air of European chic.

For all its emerging culture vultures, Glasgow's guys and gals still know how to party. Glaswegians have an uncompromising approach to work and play, which shines through on a night out in Glasgow. It may feel brutal in the short term, but just think of the stories you'll be able to tell about Wee Jakey McCafferty and his epic dog–paddle across the river.

Glasgow has all the fun, without the shortbread and tartan–doll tackiness of Edinburgh. Castles are overrated anyway, and over recent years the river has been set well on the road to becoming a sparkling waterway worthy of its great settlement. Mind you, we still wouldn't swim in it just yet ..

So go ye forth, hedonistic pleasure-seekers, with an Itchy guide clutched to your heaving bosom, singing, 'Ah belong tae Glasgie, dear auld Glasgic toon'.

Two hours in Glasgow

You're obviously in a bit of a hurry so start yourself off in George Square, right in the centre of town. Merchant city is in your sights and the sophisticated shops of the Italian Centre and Candleriggs will help you part with plenty of money in the shortest possible space of time. After all, word on the street is that Glasgow is now the second best city for shopping in Britain.

If you want to stay on the shopping theme then visit the three main precincts: Argyle Street, Buchanan Street and Sauchiehall Street, or if you've had it with shallow commercialism then head for the Gallery of Modern Art or The Lighthouse for some cerebral stimulation. Finish off with a sly pint or two in the Horseshoe on Drury Lane, one of the city's most revered bars, or if caffeine's your beast and it's a sunny day then you can get wired in one of the street-side cafes in Royal Exchange Square.

Two hours in, and the myth of Glasgae as a place of skag addicts head-butting strangers should already be well behind you. The truth is that nae matter what you're after, this is the toon for ye.

Introduction

Two days in Glasgow

STAY – We know you'll be needing every bit of extra cash for getting reeking drunk and buying Rennie Mackintosh souvenir tea towels, but there are always balances to be struck. The Brunswick hotel will give plenty of luxury without too painful a hit on the wallet, and it's also in the vibrant Merchant City, making its reasonable rates all the more tempting.

SHOP – Glasgow has some of the best shopping in Scotland so you can stuff your holdall with as many frivolous bits as catch your eye. The Buchanan Galleries and the St Enoch Centre house all the high street regulars and Buchanan Street has a more up-market feel. For real luxury the Italian Centre and Princes Square will happily work your other half and/or bank manager into a state of nervous terror.

ATTRACTIONS – The recently re-furbished Kelvingrove Art Gallery is scheduled to open this summer, and until then the GOMA is the top spot for art lovers. Those with daisies in their hair and a camper van should make for the flora and fauna at the Botanic Gardens, and if football lights your fire, get yourself to one, or all, of the major stadia in the city: Ibrox, Celtic Park, and Hampden (which also has a great museum).

EAT – Café Gandolfi in Merchant City is a must for a relaxed meal with a truly Scottish feel. For Indian lovers, Mother India extends a warm welcome (ranging up to fiery, depending on your preference), and for upmarket seafood, Rogano wins fins down.

DRINK – If you plan to acquaint yourself with all of Glasgow's watering holes you'd be advised to book that liver transplant now, and while you're at it, you'd best ask your hospital whether they do a discount for repeat operations, as there are enough bars to rupture numerous livers here. But if you simply want to get a taste for the spirit of the city then start in Uisge Beatha for a wee dram of the golden stuff. A glass of wine with the lovely staff in Brutti Ma Buoni goes down sweetly and you'll find plenty of trendy pubs and bars all the way along Ashton Lane.

CLUB – The Arches is one of the best clubs in the city, with unbelievable acoustics and mesmerizing beats. Another place that's currently pulling in the punters is BeLo in Royal Exchange Square, and if you're lucky enough to be in the city on a Sunday then Cube's Sunday Surgery is essential for some of life's more carnal pleasures.

Havana Club

PURE

CUBA

AUTHENTIC CUBAN RUM

Please drink
our rum responsibly
drinkaware.co.uk

To experience Pure Cuba logon to pieceofhavana.com

wagamama

97-103 west george street, glasgow, G2 1PB
telephone 0141 229 1468

fast and fresh noodle and rice dishes from your favourite noodle restaurant

www.wagamama.com

positive eating + positive living

Eat

Eat

CAFÉS

The Bay Tree Café
403 Great Western Road
(0141) 334 5898

Yes, that is a signed picture of Darius Danesh behind the counter. Don't worry, you can't see it until you go up to pay, so it shouldn't put you off your food. This Middle Eastern café is very authentic, with North African, Arabic and Mediterranean dishes full of spicy, intense flavours. Kebabs – but not the nasty ones you have after a night's drinking – casseroles, snacks, stews, couscous and more. You can feel the love in the room, just like Darius.

🕒 *Mon–Sat, 9.30am–10pm;*
Sun, 9.30am–9pm
🍴 *Moroccan vegetable stew, £5.95*

Beanscene
1365 Argyle Street
(0141) 357 4340

Glasgow is now overrun by many, many branches of this now-ubiquitous chain (and probably a few more by the time you read this), which are all pretty much the same: good coffee, comfy couches, decent singer–songwritery type tunes (and occasional live-music nights), lots of newspapers to browse, and big sticky muffins. Yeah, so it's a coffee chain: which is usually the scourge of 21st-century city centres, but Starbucks this place ain't. In fact, it's so nice, you would have had to invent it yourself if someone else hadn't already.

🕒 *Mon–Sat, 8am–11pm; Sun, 9am–11pm*
🍴 *Panini, £3.95*

Café Hula
321 Hope Street
(0141) 353 1660

Tapas and sandwiches are the main daytime choices at this unique city centre enclave, opposite the Theatre Royal (which is where they got the weird skeleton model in the corner from, apparently), with more substantial Mediterranean meals at night. They believe in the 'slow food' movement, cooking things for hours to bring out the flavours, and it's got to be said that the service can be a wee bit slow, too. Also, there's no menu so sometimes ordering is a bit of a guessing game. But the food is worth it and it's mega cheap, especially for the quality.

🕒 *Mon–Fri, 8am–8pm; Sat, 8am–11pm;*
Sun, 11am–5pm
🍴 *Chickpea and chorizo stew, £6.50*

Coffee Merchant

Merchant Square, 60 Candleriggs

(0141) 552 2600

As you might well be able to guess from the name, this place does pretty much every kind of coffee you could think of, from lattes and espressos to iced frappes and mochas. There's a smattering of snacks too, of the panini/bagel/sandwich variety, or nachos. But really they're only there to soak up the coffee. Which is a good thing, because after a few of their espressos you'll be jittering your way down the road like a pensioner with a nervous problem who's just seen Blair Witch for the first time. And we're not talking about Cherie.

🕒 *Mon–Fri, 8am–8pm; Sat–Sun, 10am–6pm*

🍴 *Nachos with roast vegetables, £4.95*

Grassroots Café

97 St George's Road

(0141) 333 0534

Long–established veggie café which proves there's no need to just recycle the old nutroast/vegeburger staples that others offer as the token non–meat choice by catering to non-veggie vegetable lovers. Heaps of choice and daily specials, in a comfy, arty atmosphere with a choice of cramped booths, squashy sofa or tables to sit and read your Guardian while you munch (Sun readers probably should probably steer clear, as should Clarkson fans, as gags about Guardian-reading veggie-munchers are unlikely to go down well).

🕒 *Mon–Fri, 10am–9.45pm; Sat–Sun, 10am–3.45pm & 5pm–10pm*

🍴 *Full veggie breakfast, £5.50*

Naked Soup

106 Byres Road

(0141) 334 6200

Okay, so you might think a shop which basically sells soup, soup and more soup is boring. But it's so not. Every day they make several varieties of fresh soup with all-natural ingredients, in unusual combinations. It comes served in super-nifty takeaway cartons (not those rubbish paper cups you get elsewhere) or you can eat in, perched on stools, when it comes with bread and fruit. They also do great casseroles and cakes. Mobbed at lunchtimes and sometimes a limited choice left in the afternoons.

🕒 *Mon–Fri, 9am–5pm; Sat, 10am–5pm; Sun, 11am–5pm*

🍴 *Lentil, sweet potato and coconut soup, £3*

Eat

Tchai Ovna

42 Otago Lane
(0141) 357 4524

Wonderful hippyish place known to regulars as the 'Magic Tearoom' – and indeed, it is a bit like some sort of fairytale place that Florence and Dougal would frequent. A massive variety of teas are the main attraction but the wholesome, cheap food is pretty good too. They have regular acoustic sessions and spoken word events. Easily-shocked types may freak out when they see the large hookahs, but it's all legit: fruit tobacco only. The West End branch overlooks the river, with a lovely outdoor area strung with fairy lights, while the Southside one has regular record sales.

☺ *Mon–Sun, 11am–11pm*

⑪ *Thai red curry, £5*

Tinderbox

189 Byres Road
(0141) 339 3108

This cappucino place is oh-so-achingly hip – in a sort of Eighties yuppie way, but then the Eighties are back, aren't they? You half expect to see David Beckham propping up the counter with his Real Madrid mates, as it's a bit poncey, to be honest, but the great location that it's set in means that you can watch people go by on Byres Road and see if you spot anyone you know, and laugh at people you don't. Or if you're having a bad day, you can laugh at people you do know. Just don't expect them to pop in for a chat.

☺ *Mon–Sat, 7.15am–11pm;*
Sun, 7.45am–11pm

⑪ *Fruit pie slice, £2*

Willow Tea Rooms

97 Buchanan Street
(0141) 204 5242

A Glasgow institution since the days Charles Rennie Mackintosh designed them, this tourist trap coasts by on its beautiful Art Deco and the fact that most patrons are here on holiday and therefore it's not worth the trouble to make them want to return. The food is the nastiest end of Scottich cuisine, lazily cooked and often underdone, and the prices reflect its reputation as a place for the Miss Jean Brodies of the world. Avoid, unless your granny is coming to town and wants to take a trip back in time.

☺ *Mon–Sat, 9am–4.45pm;*
Sun, 11am–4.30pm

⑪ *Haggis, neeps and tatties, £5.75*

RESTAURANTS

Ad Lib

111 Hope Street
(0141) 248 6645

A stylish diner which could almost make you believe you were really in LA – back-room booths, classic photos on the wall and a glass ceiling to see the stars by… here's looking at you, kid. They specialise in proper, big fat juicy burgers, but there's a lot of other choice too, like greasy pork ribs and of course, splendidly fattening desserts too. With this kind of cuisine, you can really go the whole hog on the American vibe and pile on enough weight to look American, too.

🕒 *Mon–Sun, 12pm–10pm*
🍴 *Lamb and grain mustard burger, £8.50*
💰 *£10.50*

Arthouse Grill

129 Bath Street
(0141) 572 6002

Part of the Hotel to the Stars ™, the Arthouse Grill is as classy as Wayne 'n' Colleeeeeen are trashy. Salads, rotisseries and grills feature prominently and the food is of excellent quality, but it's the service that really stands out. Far too often, classy joints like this take pride in intimidating the likes of us non toffs, but the Arthouse staff are friendly and helpful, making this one of Glasgow's top venues for eating out, and you can rest assured that you're not going to be encountering the Rooneys here at any point soon.

🕒 *Mon–Sun, 7am–11pm*
🍴 *Teppanyaki (five courses), £29.95*
💰 *£13.50*

Arisaig

5 Byres Road
(0141) 339 8511

If Arisaig was an instrument, it would be a refined, melancholic fiddle played on the banks of Loch Lomond by an aged, kilt–sporting Highlander. Old–school Scottish fare – from oatmeal & heather-honey flapjacks to vegetarian haggis – is served in unpretentious surroundings in both the West End and Merchant City branches of this local favourite. The emphasis lies on fresh, natural ingredients and substantial portions of the tasty food. Any Scottish granny worth her salt would approve heartily.

🕒 *Mon–Sun, 12pm–3pm & 5pm–10pm*
🍴 *Venison sausages, £12.95*
💰 *£11*

Eat

Ashoka Ashton Lane

19 Ashton Lane
(0800) 195 3195

The best feature of this restaurant is its proximity to all the pubs and boozers in Ashton Lane, so you can move from meal to piss-up almost as quickly as you'll move from upright to horizontal later on. A little on the dark and dingy side, there is an almost dungeon-esque feel to it – the cheerful staff are perhaps the only real source of light you're going to get in here. The prices are spot on though and the dark setting makes this an ideal place for a first date with a munter. Oh, and the food's bloody good, too.

- ● *Mon–Sat, 12pm–12am; Sun, 5pm–12am*
- ⓘ *Chicken tikka masala, £7.95*
- ● *£11.95*

The Bothy

11 Ruthven Lane
(0141) 334 4040

Irn-Bru sorbet and open goat's cheese pie are just a couple of the revised classics on Bothy's menu. A West End favourite, it treads the fine line between celebrating Scottish heritage and outright parody, managing to stay, thankfully, on the side of the former. Mismatched chairs, cosy wood interiors and stark white walls offset the stuffed dead things and be-kilted waiting staff. In addition to the quirkier dishes are more traditional meals, including haggis, neeps and tatties as well as trifle.

- ● *Mon–Sun, 12pm–10pm*
- ⓘ *Lewis scallops, £6.95*
- ● *£10.95*

The Cabin

996–998 Dumbarton Road
(0141) 569 1036

A wee bit off the beaten track in the wilds of Partick (eek, shudder etc), but worth the trip for the fab grub and the nice people. Looks like a ship's cabin, but they serve nicer stuff than mouldy biscuits and grog (or whatever Johnny Depp lived on in that pirate movie), like seafood and lamb. The waitress, a lady named Wilma, is a bit of a star – she was on a local TV documentary a while back about her trip to sing cabaret in Las Vegas. Get her to sing to you while you eat.

- ● *Tue–Thu & Sun, 12pm–2.30pm & 4.30pm–9.30pm; Fri–Sat, 12pm–2.30pm & 4.30pm–9pm*
- ⓘ *Set lunch, £9*
- ● *£12*

Café Andaluz

2 Cresswell Lane

(0141) 339 1111

Deep in the basement of Cresswell Lane lie more tempting tapas than you could shake a maraca at. Intimate surrounding, complete with sofas and scatter cushions, make for a relaxed atmosphere, ideal for the caring sharing nature of tapas. Occasionally verging on the pricey – over £4 for four prawns? – the food is great quality, making the prices hard to resent. Goat's cheese with marmalade perfectly mixes cloying heaviness with refreshing sweetness, while the honey–battered chicken is enough to give deep-fat-frying a good name.

🕒 *Mon–Sat, 12pm–11pm; Sun, 12.30pm–10.30pm*

🍴 *Seafood paella, £9.45*

💰 *£10.95*

Café Gandolfi

64 Albion Street

(0141) 552 6813

One of the best restaurants/bars/bistros/whatevers in town: FACT. Classy but unpretentious, fancy dishes but also homely Scottish staples (smokies or haggis, neeps and tatties), a fab bar upstairs, a restaurant that's equally good for a casual lunch with friends or with someone you need to impress and the prices – well, they're not café cheap but they're not too bad. Give it a go. No relation to that old beardy bloke from Lord Of The Rings, by the way.

🕒 *Mon–Sat, 9am–11.30pm; Sun, 12pm–11.30pm*

🍴 *Arbroath smokies, £5.10*

💰 *£11.20*

Café Cossachok

10 King Street

(0141) 553 0733

Proving there's more to Russian food than cabbage, beetroot and vodka, this wee place is a bit of Eastern Europe transplanted west and frequented by many ex-pats. There's a little art gallery above the dining area and live music on Sundays – just don't get carried away and start doing the Cossack dance. As well as obvious stuff like borscht, blinis and stroganoff, it's worth trying some of their more unfamiliar dishes drawn from the countries of the former Soviet Union.

🕒 *Tue–Thu, 11.30am–9pm; Fri–Sun, 4pm–11pm*

🍴 *Moscow blintzes, £7.25*

💰 *£10.95*

Eat

Canton Express

407 Sauchiehall Street
(0141) 332 0145

Canton Express is slightly surreal with its blinding fluorescent lights and black vinyl benches. Its main clientele (drunken students emerging from the Garage nightclub with the munchies) swear by its budget menu and late opening hours. Take a table by the window, watch the world stagger by and attempt to decipher the wall-mounted Chinese menu for real comedy value. With all the popular favourites including beef chow mein and chicken curry, this is fast food at its best, and at its most brilliantly basic. Head on down.

⊚ Mon–Sun, 12pm–4am
⓪ Chicken curry, £4.50

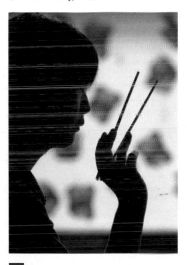

The City Merchant

97 Candleriggs
(0141) 553 1577

The City Merchant might well look like a cosy pub, but is frequented by a business-y crowd, and is also a cracking place to go and sample the delights of the sea. Their fish and seafood is all very fresh, with daily specials and everything from lobster to lemon sole. While you tuck in, reflect smugly on how you're being really altruistic: £1 of every bill goes to the Glasgow Old People's Welfare Association. So not only can you sit and stuff your face with trout, you can help to feed an old trout too.

⊚ Mon–Sat, 12pm–10.30pm
⓪ Grilled trout fillet, £7.50
⊘ £13.75

Dakhin

89 Candleriggs
(0141) 553 2585

A homesick Sri Lankan friend of Itchy's once started crying in Dakhin because the dishes so reminded her of her childhood. Everyone else will be delighted by the fabulously unusual and restrained food here, which is based more on South Indian (and Sri Lankan) cuisine than the Northern or Bangladeshi style that you find elsewhere. Things are subtler, with coconut flavours and tomato sauces. They give you plenty of extras too, like the huge dosas (a sort of light pancake bread) for all to share. Reasonable prices too.

⊚ Mon–Fri, 12pm–2pm & 5pm–10.30pm; Sat–Sun, 1pm–10.30pm
⓪ Kozhi melagu chettinard, £10.25
⊘ £12

Ding's Grand Buffet

29 Albion Street

(0141) 552 5115

It's a buffet, it's pretty grand and ding! goes the till as it racks up the bill that is a little bit pricier than elsewhere, which varies depending on the time of day. There's a whole host of choices of meat, fish and vegetable dishes, which are all well-cooked and crispy, delicately flavoured and filling. Plus, for the more adventurous readers out there, if you can cope with the unusual smell, the coconut jelly dessert will slip down easily afterwards. Get slurping, kids.

📽 *Mon–Thu, 12pm–10.30pm; Fri–Sat, 12pm–12am*

🍴 *Dinner buffet, £12.50*

💰 *£10.50*

Gumbo

33 Ingram Street

(0141) 552 2929

A weird mix of party bar (with karaoke on Friday and Saturdays) and gourmet joint (they've won several local restaurant awards), this place is influenced by Louisiana and the 'Let the good times roll' philosophy of New Orleans. Which means that as well as trad American dishes, you get things like jambalaya (cod fish pie, me oh my oh), spicy gumbo (hence the name) and Cajun pork. Seafood is big here, too. You might be too by the time you leave.

📽 *Tue–Thu, 12pm–10.30pm; Fri–Sat, 12pm–11pm; Sun, 12pm–10pm*

🍴 *Gumbo stove pot (to share), £16*

💰 *£ 7.95*

Ichiban Noodle Café

184 Dumbarton Road

(0141) 334 9222

Even that stroppy chick in the schoolgirl outfit from *Kill Bill* would be happy with the way things are run here. With an impressive menu, Ichiban caters to Glasgow's more ambitious sushi enthusiasts as well as keeping curry lovers happy. For the quality of the dishes, the prices are very reasonable, and what with the friendly warm service, you'd have to have sushi between your ears not to appreciate eating a meal here.

📽 *Mon–Wed, 12pm–10pm; Thu–Sat, 12pm–11pm; Sun, 1pm–10pm*

🍴 *Beef curry with chargrilled sirloin steak, £6.90*

💰 *£9*

Eat

Khublai Khan

26 Candleriggs

(0141) 552 5646

Eat like the Mongols – but without having to wear those massive fur coats and pointy helmets. Unless you really want to, in which case this is the perfect place to try out your best Genghis Khan get up. Pick your food (usually meat) and get the chef to cook it on a hotplate meant to emulate the shields of the Khan's warriors held over campfires. Different, eh? It's fun trying a selection of exotic meats like zebra, springbok and shark as well as the usual – find out if they really all taste like chicken.

🕒 Mon–Sun, 5pm–11am

🍴 All-you-can-eat barbecue, £17.95

💷 £11.99

Loon Fung

417–419 Sauchiehall Street

(0141) 332 1477

No, smartass, you don't have to be a Loon to eat here. Nor does it help. The décor looks like a set from *Hero* or *House of Flying Daggers*, all deep, rich colours and dragons. But there is no wire-fu here and the waiters walk to your table, without gliding through the air, to deliver some tasty dim sum, prepared on the premises. Very popular with the local Chinese community, which is an endorsement in itself surely. If you don't eat here, you're a loony.

🕒 Mon–Sat, 12pm–11.30pm; Sun, 11.30am–11.30pm

🍴 Set lunch, £5.30

💷 £16 (1 litre)

Mao

84 Brunswick Street

(0141) 564 5161

It's funny how there isn't a Russian restaurant called Stalin's, or a German one called Hitler... well, politics aside, this is a very trendy fusion joint featuring not just Chinese food but a variety of Asian dishes. Huge paintings of Chairman Mao dominate the room like Big Brother (the government in the Orwell novel, not the one that has wannabe popstars/tv presenters tormenting each other on live tv), as if frowning on your Western decadence as you tuck into the large portions. A bit pretentious, but a top-notch menu.

🕒 Mon–Sun, 12pm–11pm

🍴 Five-spice chicken, £9.50

💷 £12.50

Mono

12 Kings Court, King Street

(0141) 553 2400

Think of vegans and the uninformed might think of strange bean-munching, sack-wearing social rejects who live in a caravan with too many cats. Yet Mono, Scotland's only vegan café, manages to combine the requirements of not eating any bits of animals with refreshing coolness and a lack of pretension, making it suitable for crusties and meat-eaters alike. Vegan burgers, potato cakes and Thai curry contradict the image of vegan food as bland and the homemade lemonade is possibly Glasgow's best-kept secret.

🕓 *Sun–Thu, 12pm–12am; Fri–Sat, 12pm–1am*
🍴 *Tofu and vegetable satay, £7.25*
💲 *£9.95*

OKO

The Todd Building, 68 Ingram Street

(0141) 572 1500

Conveyer-belt cuisine – somehow it's so much more exciting than queuing up for school dinners, even though the principle is sorta the same. You go up, grab your condiments, napkins etc, then just pick up whatever dish you fancy as they rotate round. You're charged depending on the colour–coded empty plates at the end; lime plates are £1.25, white bowls are £4.75 and so on. More than 60 varieties of sushi including some really weird-looking ones and they'll also make stuff on request.

🕓 *Tue–Thu, 12pm–3pm & 6pm–11pm;*
Fri–Sat, 12pm–12am; Sun, 5pm–11pm
🍴 *All–you–can–eat nights (check dates), £15*
💲 *£11.95*

Mr Singh's India

149 Eldersie Street

(0141) 204 0186

Mr Singh's India is an upmarket place that is popular with footballers and their wives (or mistresses). By which, we mean the restaurant. Not some kind of renegade state that the proprietor's set up. The staff are kilt-wearing, Scottish Asians, which is cute. This place may well be quite posh and a bit pricier than some, but the food is good and the service excellent. Haggis pakora is their notable dish, summing up the fusion of the two cultures nicely. They also do many dishes from the Jaipur area.

🕓 *Mon–Sat, 12pm–12am; Sun, 2.30pm–12am*
🍴 *Karahi chicken, £8.95*
💲 *£9.95*

Eat

Oran Mor

731–735 Great Western Road
(0141) 357 6226

An old, converted church at the corner of Great Western and Byres Roads. Upstairs there's a crazy, Sistine Chapel type ceiling painted by genius novelist/artist Alasdair Gray. In the basement they do this great 'a pie, a play and a pint' thing at lunch. In the middle lies a big bar which gets packed at weekends, and there's a slightly cheesy club downstairs, too. Don't overlook the brasserie round the side (posh, pricey, quality) or the wee conservatory tacked onto the other side (nice for lunch, airy, bright). You could spend your whole day and night here.

🕒 *Mon–Sun, 12pm–10pm*
🍴 *Canon of venison, £19.50*
💷 *£12.50*

Roastit Bubbly Jocks

450 Dumbarton Road
(0141) 339 3355

Who with the what now? For all the Sassenachs out there who haven't got a clue what this place is named after (or just those without couthy old relatives), the name means 'roast turkey'. And lo! There, er, wasn't any on the menu, at least there wasn't when Itchy was there. Oh well. Just have to make do with some vaguely Mediterranean flavours and daily fish specials then. Which is by no means a hardship. Quite often packed and noisy, but jolly with it.

🕒 *Tue–Thu, 5pm–10pm; Fri–Sun,*
12pm–2.30pm & 5.30pm–10pm
🍴 *Seafood platter, £6.95*
💷 *£10*

The Rogano

11 Exchange Place
(0141) 248 4055

The Rogano is a city centre institution with the kind of art deco design that makes you feel like you're a major player in an old movie, about to sip cocktails with Cary Grant or Rita Hayworth. Unfortunately, the customers aren't quite up to the same levels of glamour as Cary or Rita, but nonetheless, it's still a pretty posh crowd, though the downstairs café is younger and hipper. The food is mostly traditional dishes with a wide range of seafood.

🕒 *Mon–Sun, 12pm–2.30pm*
& 6.30pm–10.30pm
🍴 *Daily fish grill, £9.50*
💷 *£16*

Shanghai Shufflo

256 Bath Street
(0141) 572 0888

Shanghai's appeal is found in its comedy factor. Surrounded by karaoke chaos, alcohol-fuelled guests are encouraged to grab a mic and warble the night away in a tacky-tuned frenzy, complete with '70s-style wigs and party poppers. General merriment overshadows the food, but who cares when you can grab an Afro wig and join in the confusion? Portions are fairly small but the fixed-price menu is reasonable at £12 a head Sundays to Wednesdays. Get a crowd of mates together, stuff the noodles in, squeeze onto the dance floor and shake your stuff.

🕒 *Tue–Sun, 5pm–10pm*
🍴 *Set dinner & karaoke, price varies*
🍷 *£18.50 (1 litre)*

Stravaigin

28 Gibson Street
(0141) 334 2665

A reliable and never stodgy institution, which is doing its damnedest to take over the city, and rightly so. There's the bar on Gibson Street, the restaurant underneath and a smaller bistro on Ruthven Lane (off Byres Road). Their motto is 'think global, eat local' which means that they take a load of Scottish ingredients, and then they give them exotic twists, but not just for the sake of it – they work, and they work pretty damn well. Nice staff, nice surroundings, nice food. In a word, fanbloodytastic.

🕒 *Tue–Thu, 5pm–11pm; Fri–Sun,*
12pm–2.30pm & 5pm–11pm
🍴 *Thai duck and scallop red curry, £15.50*

Sizzler's Steak House

79 Albion Street
(0141) 552 4200

They claim to be Glasgow's only original steakhouse and to be inspired by the 'sophisticated supper clubs' of the '40s and '50s. Whatever they were – going by this, they seem to have been places where people had to wear jackets and ties (er, the men) on Fridays and Saturdays, where everyone loved meat and had no fears of BSE, CJD or cholesterol and where the atmosphere was terribly, terribly elegant. Bit pricey and definitely not for vegetarians.

🕒 *Mon–Sat, 12pm–2pm & 6pm–10pm;*
Sun, 6pm–10pm
🍴 *Chargrilled sizzler, £23*
🍷 *£11*

Eat

Two Fat Ladies

88 Dumbarton Road
(0141) 339 1944

Nothing to do with those two game old girls on the motorbike and sidecar who used to have that cookery show on the TV – it's a bingo reference (88, geddit?). Your number could be up here, if you're looking for a cosy (for which read totally cramped, but not unpleasantly so) little neighbourhood restaurant with fine fish and seafood presented exquisitely. As Itchy went to press, they were planning to open a spin-off at Blythswood Square. Three fat ladies, then.

◉ *Mon–Sat, 12pm–3pm & 5pm–10.30pm; Sun, 5pm–10pm*
🍴 *Two courses, £10.95*
💷 *£11.50*

Wagamama

97–103 West George Street
(020) 70093600

For reasonably priced, cheerful and very delicious Japanese food, Wagamama cannot be bettered. Even novices to this ethnic genre can find something they enjoy (and don't fear, chopsticks are not obligatory) in the range of thick or thin noodles, sweet or sour soups and spicy or mild curries. A cosy atmosphere prevails given the long bench seating arrangements and constant hum of lots of satisfied customers–this place is always busy and for a very good reason. It's great. Go. Nuff said.

◉ *Mon–Sat, 12pm–11pm; Sun, 12.30pm–10pm*
🍴 *Chicken kare lomen, £7.25*
💷 *£10.95*

The Wee Curry Shop

23 Ashton Lane
(0141) 357 5280

Not for the claustrophobic – it really is wee. As in tiny, toty, ickle, weeny. Both branches are small and intimate affairs, so you probably don't want to take someone there to talk secrets. You'll be too busy eating to talk anyway, as the small size does at least mean that the chef isn't rushed or dealing with too many customers' orders to give each meal personal attention.

◉ *Mon–Thu, 12.30pm–2.30pm & 5.30pm–10.30pm; Fri, 12.30pm–2.30pm & 5.30pm–11pm; Sat, 12.30pm–11pm; Sun, 3pm–11pm*
🍴 *Set lunch, £4.75*
💷 *£11.50*

FOOD FOR THOUGHT

ITCHY'S GUIDE TO FOODS THAT EVERYONE SHOULD TRY AT LEAST ONCE. GO ON, BE ADVENTUROUS. WE DARES YOU...

Chocolate insects

Lovingly enveloped in a layer of chocolatey goodness, upmarket food stores have recently started selling these critters. You can choose from scorpion lollies or locust chews. Think, 'I'm a celebrity, get me into these...'

Offal

While meat hysteria in the wake of the BSE crisis might discourage you from trying offal, don't be put off. Offal comes in all shapes and sizes, and although not all of you will be up to the test of courage presented by sweetbreads (glands), things such as pan–fried chicken livers are more than palatable.

Kangaroo fillet

Whilst this steak–like meat can be a bit chewy, it's very lean and low–cholesterol. What's more, for the environmentally conscious amongst you, it may ease your conscience to know that they're not endangered and that farming them causes less damage to the environment than the farming of traditional animals. Available from your local Walkabout.

Haggis

Take some heart, liver and lungs; mince with onion, oatmeal, suet, spices and salt. Boil in a sheep's stomach lining for several hours, and you have Scotland's most traditional dish. To not eat it would be cultural snobbery.

Jellied eels

These little tubs of gunk are packed with so much Cockney authenticity that eating just a couple will give you the same level of East End cred as a Pearly King/Queen. Tastes like poached salmon. In slime.

Itchy

BALTIS IN BIRMINGHAM?
COCKTAILS IN CARDIFF?
GIGS IN GLASGOW?

IF YOU'RE STARTING FROM
SCRATCH, YOU'D BETTER
GET ITCHY.

FOR THE BEST THAT
THE UK HAS TO OFFER,
LOG ON TO

WWW.ITCHYCITY.CO.UK

Bath, Birmingham, Brighton, Bristol, Cambridge, Cardiff,
Edinburgh, Glasgow, Leeds, Liverpool, London, Manchester,
Nottingham, Oxford, Sheffield, York

Drink

Drink

BARS

Air Organic

36 Kelvingrove Street

(0141) 564 5200

Bohemians will enjoy Air Organic's slouchy/effortless attitude and people with good cheekbones and Levi's ad hairstyles will fit right in. There's a focus on organic ingredients, but either way that's more relevant in the upstairs restaurant that costs too much for us plebs. Back to the point: the sort of lo-fi décor and demeanour that sum up the West End at its best, basically.

⊛ *Sun–Thu, 11am–11pm; Fri & Sat, 11am–12am; Food, Mon–Sun, 12pm 9pm*

⑪ *Burger and chips, £6.95*

✪ *£11.95*

The Arches Café Bar

253 Argyle Street

(0141) 565 1035

Through the Argyle Street entrance, down the foyer, hang a right and descend: the café bar bit of the massive theatre-meets-live-music-cum-art-space-with-adjoining über-club that is The Arches attracts all the folk who're here for the other stuff. Cutting-edge, visual art types happily mingle with business lunchers (at lunchtime) and pre-clubbers (er, before the clubs open …) in a high-roofed, open-plan and modern bar with a chic, seafood-orientated menu. Cool without developing an attitude problem.

⊛ *Mon–Sat, 11am–12am; Sun, 12pm–2am; Food, Mon–Sat, 12pm–10pm; Sun, 12.30pm–10pm*

⑪ *Fresh Scottish seafood fajitas, £9.95*

✪ *£9.50*

moskito BAR & BITES
200 Bath Street, Glasgow G2 4HG
T : 0141 331 1777, F : 0141 353 3851

Bar Buddha

142 St Vincent Street

(0141) 248 7881

The fat golden fellow in the window has spread his seed over the last few years, with Buddhas in the West End, Southside and up Sauchiehall Street. This is the original, right in the heart of the finance district and popular with good-looking sorts who appreciate the eastern promise and cheeky cocktail menu, and the intimate little club downstairs. You can imagine the *Sex & The City* gals drinking here… when they were young … and the show was funny.

🕐 *Mon–Sat, 12pm–2am; Sun, 12pm–12am; Food, 12pm–10pm*

🍴 *Thai green chicken curry, £6.95*

🍷 *£9.95*

Bar Oz

499 Great Western Road

(0141) 334 0884

Do you like football and rugby? You'd better. Bar Oz is that sort of place: the antipodean theme (paraphernalia on the walls, Foster's on tap, big, hunky portions) tends to appeal to the jocks from nearby student accommodation and Glasgow University itself. And it's bloody good at what it does: lots of seats, lots of viewing points for the TVs, and a well-stocked, well-tended bar.

🕐 *Sun–Thu, 12.30pm–11pm; Fri & Sat, 12pm–12am; Food, 12.30pm–7pm*

🍴 *Basic burger and chips, £2.45*

🍷 *£7.70*

Bar Soba

11 Mitchell Lane

(0141) 204 2404

Popular Japanese, fusion-food hangout sitting beside The Lighthouse art project, and one of the nearest bars to the big Buchanan Street shops. Thirsty shoppers like popping in here, perhaps for the muted colours and deftly balanced angles that suggest feng–shui was as much a consideration as sushi when they designed it. There's some cool beer on offer, but seating gets a bit tight at times.

🕐 *Mon–Sat, 10am–12am; Sun, 12pm–12am; Food, Mon–Sun, 12pm–10pm*

🍴 *Yakitori pork skewers, £7.95*

🍷 *£9.75*

Due to last year's re-jigging of licensing hours, you can get a drink up to the closing times listed, but you might get some bonus drinking time too. Result! **Itchy**

Drink

Brel

39–43 Ashton Lane
(0141) 342 4966

Why's there a big picture of Humphrey Bogart on the wall? Oh, it's Jacques Brel, the Belgian chanteur. And it's a Belgian bar. Which is why it's called Brel. Ah, it all makes sense now. Well, it's better than 'Van Damme's Alehouse' or 'Bar Tintin', no? There's an impressive stock of beers from the homeland and the best steak in the city. Gourmet sausages and mussels pop up as well. The best feature is the beer garden though, whose view in summer is stunning.

◉ *Mon–Sat, 11am–12am; Sun, 12.30pm–12am; Food, Mon–Fri, 12pm–3pm 5pm–10.30pm; Sat & Sun, 12pm–10.30pm*
🍴 *Pot of mussels and chips, £9.95*
🍷 *£9.50*

Brunswick Cellars

239 Sauchiehall Street
(0141) 332 9329

Dark and homely (quite possibly the darkest bar in Glasgow, in fact); Full of character (candles on big wooden tables); music orientated (millions of gig and club-night posters near the entrance, and proper local DJs every night); Sneaky on a Sunday when they do four pint pitchers for a fiver and you go down during the day and hours pass and you come out and it's dark and you're drunk but it's ok because you spent less than twenty quid but it's not ok because you've got to get up in six hours. Phew.

◉ *Mon–Sat, 12pm–12am; Sun, 1pm–12am; Food, Mon–Sun, 12pm–3pm*
🍴 *Burger and chips, £3.95*
🍷 *£7*

Brutti ma Buoni

106 Brunswick Street

(0141) 552 0001

Sleek greys and long, flowing lines, it's also the residents' bar of the adjoining and rather hotshot Brunswick Hotel. So, it would seem that 'brutti ma buoni' (which translates as 'ugly but good', cunning linguists) more likely describes the pizzas – crazy little misshapen nutters – than the watering hole itself. Fear not – they pass the taste test with flying colours, as does all the food on the witty and damned cheap menu. Merchant City fashionistas provide the clientele. What's Italian for 'the proof of the pizza is in the eating?'.

Ⓒ Mon–Sun, 12pm–12am; Food, Mon–Sat, 12pm–9pm; Sun, 12pm–8pm

Ⓘ Steak baguette, £6.50

Firewater

341 Sauchiehall Street

(0141) 354 0350

Doesn't quite do what it says on the tin – thankfully, because what it says on the tin (or the sign on the entrance at least) is 'Real Music, Hard Liquor', which conjures up images of big bikers supping Wild Turkey. Instead we have a gigantic drinking den for the discerning student and the guitar music fan. A 'Super–Indie Pub', if you will. Movies play silently on the plasma screen – sit there long enough and you'll undoubtedly catch 'Scarface' as 'Fools Gold' booms out the speakers.

Ⓒ Mon–Sat, 12pm–12am; Sun, 12.30pm–12am; Food, Mon–Wed, 12pm–3pm; Thu–Sun, 12pm–5pm

Ⓘ 10-inch tortizza, £3.95

Ⓕ £8.95

Bunker

100 100 Bath Street

(0141) 229 1427

Quite why Bunker is so called is unclear. Thankfully this gigantic bar makes no effort to resemble anything which we might associate with bunkers: no sand or golf balls, no emergency supplies for the nuclear holocaust. If any bar were to be a nuclear bunker, mind you, this would be a good bet: free Internet access at the back, free pool at the front, free live music on a Wednesday and free beer from the bar. (OK, the beer costs you – but if there were a nuclear holocaust it would be free, surely?)

Ⓒ Mon–Sat, 12pm–12am; Sun, 12.30pm–12am; Food, Mon–Sat, 12pm–9pm; Sun, 11.30am–9pm

Ⓘ Bangers'n mash, £7.25

Ⓕ £9

Drink

Moskito

200 Bath Street
(0141) 331 1777

There's a nice Mediterranean vibe going on in Moskito, with the stone floors, the cool blues and aquamarines and the laid-back house music all contributing to its relaxed demeanour. The good-looking staff serve good-looking customers of the streetwise and trendy variety. Well worth munching in as well, with an appropriately Greek-influenced menu featuring dishes like feta parcels with a tsatziki dip.

© *Mon–Sat, 12pm–12am; Sun, 12.30pm–12am; Food, Mon–Sat, 12pm–9pm; Sun, 12pm–6pm*

⓪ *Chilli and chips, £5.95*

❷ *£9.95*

Over the Road

207 Bath Street
(0141) 248 2123

Turn ye back, oh Edinburgh posers, for this place is definitely not a style bar. So all of you auld reekie fancy dans'll have to check your mullet at the cloak-room if you want to enjoy the homely pleasures of this leather-couched watering hole, trendsters. Grub like ma used to make it, a relaxed atmosphere and the odd open mic night keep this bar's unpretentious crowd happy as larry. But hold yer horses there, just 'cos they're not pretentious, doesn't mean they do Cheese. So if you're after Justin, Christine or Britney, this may not be the place for you, stilton fans.

© *Mon–Sun, 10am–12am*

Pivo Pivo

15 Waterloo Street
(0141) 564 0100

The least assuming beer hall in town, quietly pointing out on the menu that there are over 90 beers on offer: that's more than anywhere else. Deceptively big once you're down the stairs, opening up into a big room that surrounds you with Prague Square on the walls, so you feel as if you're in the middle of it... well, apart from the fact there's a dirty big screen hanging from the wall at the front showing the football. But that's not a bad thing. Also has the most dapper bouncer in Glasgow.

© *Mon–Sat, 12pm–12am; Sun, 12.30pm–12am; Food, Mon–Sat, 12pm–7pm; Sun, 12.30pm–6pm*

⓪ *Fajitas, £8.95 (2-for-1 all the time)*

❷ *£9.95*

Republic Biere Halle

9 Gordon Street

(0141) 204 0706

Probably the best of the various 'beer halls' that Glasgow has given birth to these last couple of years, two of which are sister venues to this. Brutal, urban design (think right angles everywhere) plays host to a menu boasting 'over 90 beers from around the world' and although you'll pay about three quid for most of them, that's fair enough when you find yourself thinking 'I could really do with a Trappist dark ale brewed to a centuries old recipe in a monastery outside Antwerp, right about now…' As you do.

Ⓒ Mon–Sat, 12pm–12am; Sun, 12.30pm–12am; Food, Mon–Sun, 12pm–10pm

Ⓘ Wood-fired pizzas, £7.50

Ⓩ £9.95

Revolution

K7–K9 Renfield Street

(0141) 331 2614

As a bar it's alright: modern, comfortable-meets-cool, attracting folk from the Odeon cinema that faces it. As a vodka bar it's fantastic, with a (theft–worthy) menu giving the history of the spirit and offering enlightening descriptions of what you're supposed to detect in the aftertaste of each one. Bison grass vodka and apple juice is a favourite. And the homemade flavoured vodkas (many varieties) are a clever way to get shitfaced at the bar while maintaining a façade of sophistication that blue aftershock just won't give.

Ⓒ Mon–Sat, 12pm–12am; Sun, 1pm–12pm; Food, Mon–Sat, 12pm–7pm; Sun, 1pm–7pm

Ⓘ Revolution club sandwich, £3.50

Drink

Russell's Café Bar

77 Byres Road
(0141) 334 7132

The best bits of the bar/pub/café mix. So many good points: dark, homely, warm, plasma screens showing sport, a proper chef cooking about 50 different dishes from an incredibly comprehensive menu, the best tomato ketchup in Glasgow (seriously), a good chance of getting a booth seat, opens up into Byres Road in the warm weather, licensed until 1am if you buy food. Go.

⏰ *Mon–Thu, 11.30am–11pm; Fri & Sat, 11.30am–12pm, Sun, 12.30pm–11pm; Food, Mon–Sat, 11am–11.30pm; Sun, 12pm–11.30pm;*

🍴 *Haggis pizza, £6.50*

💰 *£9.25*

Saint Jude's

190 Bath Street
(0141) 352 8800

One of the first really suave joints on Bath Street, the last in a 100-odd metre stretch that's got all the hotshot ones. Saint Jude's design is vaguely like those Sixties interpretations of what the 'space age' might look like, without entering kitsch territory... no, the media darlings and well-to-do regulars would not want that. They keep Saint Jude's consistently popular, with regulars especially fond of the simple but incredibly well-made cocktails. It's a good place to be seen, if that's your scene.

⏰ *Mon–Sat, 12pm–12am; Food, Mon–Sat, 12pm–7pm*

🍴 *Tiger-prawn stir-fry, £5.50*

💰 *£14*

The Solid Rock Café
19 Hope Street
(0141) 221 1105

It's an institution, this one. 'The Solid' really is where to go if you want cheap booze and proper, heavy rock. Goths, metalheads and anyone in between will frequent it and its lack of pretension is why it's so well thought of. If you've ever moshed, muchuga'd or made the devil's horn sign without being ironic then you have to have a pint here. It's the rules. Although if you've never done any of the above, then this may not be the right place for you.

Mon–Sat ,11am–12am; Sun, 12.30pm–12am; Food, Mon–Sat, 12–7; Sun, 1pm–7pm
Chicken fajitas, £4.95
£8

Stavka
373 377 Sauchiehall Street
(0141) 333 3940

It's easy to see why Stavka has been such a success story. A classily executed Russian theme, a (seriously) gigantic screen for major football games, an immensely popular cocktail bar upstairs and Baltica beer on tap all add to its stock. Indeed, the bar's popularity allows the door staff to be rather discerning, so make a bit of an effort with your look if you want in – the 'Absinthe Appletini' is worth it. The 'traditional Russian pie' with fish and egg, perhaps, not so much.

Mon–Sun 11am–12pm; Food, Mon–Sat, 12pm–12am; Sun, 12pm–6pm
Beef stroganoff, £9.95
£9.75

Tron Theatre
63 Trongate
(0141) 552 8587

Fear not – being the adjoining bar to the Tron Theatre doesn't propel the luvvie-count into levels where you want to scream, stand up and fling your pint of Peroni over the nearest bearded man with a neckerchief (though that might be fun). There's a great vibe here. Folk pop in for a beer and a read of the paper at the minimalist bar up front, while hungry pre-theatre punters head for the converted church behind, to stuff themselves on fine Scottish/European dishes by candlelight.

Mon–Sat, 10am–12am; Sun, 11am–12am; Food, Mon–Sat, 12pm–11pm
Smoked chicken and mozzarella flatbread, £6
£12.50

Drink

Underworld

95 Union Street

(0141) 221 5209

It's good to know that as soon as you disembark the train at Central you can dive into the ubiquitous Cooper's bar, but if you hold your horses for about 15 more seconds, Underworld's right outside. It may have been the first of the Mexican styled bars in Glasgow. You can't see much evidence of it, yet ordering a Corona with lime just feels right – easily gulped if you're leaving the city centre and your train's ten minutes away. The eating section takes the Mexican theme more seriously, though.

Ⓒ *Mon-Sat, 11am-12am; Sun, 12.30pm-12am; Food, 12pm-9.30pm*

Ⓤ *Combo fajitas, £9.95*

Ⓠ *£9.75*

Vodka Wodka

31–35 Ashton Lane

(0141) 341 0669

So good they named it twice (but once in Polish, to show off). A plethora of different types of the world's favourite spirit stand proudly behind the brushed metal bar and draw in the mid-twenties crowd, better suited to larger groups of people come evening. During the day it's a different story, kept ticking over by passing student traffic from nearby Glasgow University, sneaking in a pint before a lecture, then another few as they decide to skip the lecture.

Ⓒ *Daily, 10am-12am (licensed 'til 11pm, Mon-Sat; 'til 12.30pm Sun)*

Ⓤ *Pasta dishes, £6*

Ⓠ *£9.95*

The Universal

57 Sauchiehall Street Lane

(0141) 332 8899

Tucked just out of sight behind the Watt Bros department store, this hidden gem is one of the best bars in Glasgow and also doubles as a restaurant and club venue upstairs. The staff are laid-back and friendly, the drink is good and reasonably priced, the atmosphere is unpretentious but hip. Cool music and low lighting make it a haven from the drunken revelry that takes over the rest of Sauchiehall Street at weekends. Mind you, you still have to walk home through it, so drink up and if you can't beat 'em

Ⓒ *Mon-Sun, 12pm-12am; Food, Mon-Sat, 12pm-9pm; Sun, 12pm-8pm*

Ⓤ *Thai chicken curry, £5.95*

Ⓠ *£10.95*

Waxy O'Connor's

44 West George Street

(0141) 354 5154

Though it's hard to go wrong with an Irish pub, sometimes it's really right. Take this massive, fantastic, 'Guinness-meets-Swiss Family Robinson' creation of nooks, crannies, walkways and six (count 'em) bars. A few shandies over par and you might get lost, yes, but that's part of Waxy's charm. Get your bearings, sit down and tuck into some old-fashioned comfort food like Irish lamb stew and colcannon, or the best chowder you've ever tasted.

Ⓒ *Mon-Wed, 12pm-11pm; Thu-Sat, 12am-12am; Sun, 12.30pm-11pm; Food, 12pm-9pm*

Ⓤ *Fish & chips £6.25*

Ⓠ *£11*

PUBS

The Ark
42–46 North Frederick Street
(0141) 559 4331

One of the 'Yellow' chain of student-orientated pubs (this one even more so because of its proximity to Strathclyde University and the College of Building and Printing). A little beer garden at the back and a balcony that can be hired out are plus points; cheap but hideous cocktails start out as plus points but are very bad boys in the long run. Apart from that, it pretty much feels like a student union, puggies, pool table et al.

☺ Mon–Sat, 11am–12am; Sun, 12.30pm–12am; Food, Mon–Sat, 11am–6.45pm; Sun, 12.30pm–6.45pm

The Auctioneer's
6 North Court Street, St Vincent Place
(0141) 229 5851

The name might conjure up images of bargainous alcohol auctions, but the real beauty of this place is that it's good to know about if you're in the Buchanan Street neck of the woods, looking for a beer without wanting to deal with the potentially high arsehole-count in nearby bars like Praha or The Slug & Lettuce. Many people have similar plans to your own, so it's often pleasantly busy and chirpy. Get in there, and prepare to join the clientele in bitching about cheap leather–shoed monkeys spoiling the city centre's nightlife.

☺ Mon–Sat, 11am–12am; Sun, 12.30pm–12am; Food, Mon–Sat, 12pm–10pm; Sun, 12.30pm–9pm

Blackfriars
36 Bell Street
(0141) 552 5924

The Baby Grand Group's one and only pub venture is a young and music–centric place, with a basement section that hosts everything from jazz afternoons to techno sessions and poetry talks. The new 'gastro menu' elevates it above the rest, as does the Baltika on tap and the brilliant location in the heart of the Merchant City. Great tunes, great food and great beer make this place the absolute pick of the Baby Grand bunch. Which is nothing to do with the Brady Bunch. Just in case you weren't sure.

☺ Mon–Sat, 12pm–12am; Sun, 12.30pm–12am; Food, Mon–Sat, 12pm–8pm; Sun, 12.30pm–8pm

Drink

Captain's Rest

185 Great Western Road

(0141) 331 2722

A salty sea dog ye may not be, boyo, but ye won't find yourself being forced to walk the plank as a landlubber in the Captain's Rest. In fact, it's best if you don't mention rocking about on a turbulent sea at all, as when hardcore benders have dragged on into day two (or three) it's not uncommon to catch the practitioners winding down here, and you don't want to upset any fragile stomachs. Does a good pint. It's quiet too, and within staggering distance of a few bus stops and two metro stations. No boats, though. Darn.

🍺 *Mon–Thu, 11am–11pm; Fri & Sat, 11am–12pm; Sun, 12.30pm–11pm; Tue–Fri, 1pm–6pm; Sat & Sun, 12pm–5pm*

The Counting House

2 St. Vincent Place

(0141) 225 0160

It used to be a counting house. Coincidence? We think not. Gigantic pub that's immensely popular with an older crowd and as a meeting place for big groups. Prices are brilliant and the no-music policy has the curious effect of actually forcing you to make conversation with your drinking buddies. Weird. Dangerously, it's also one of the few pubs that will actually do you a burger, chips and a pint for not much more than a McDonald's and in not much more time either. Drunken afternoons in the office, anyone?

🍺 *Mon–Sun, 10am–12pm;*
Food, Mon–Sun, 10am–12pm

The Crystal Palace

36 Jamaica Street

(0141) 221 2624

What could so easily have been just another corporate pub with an 'old favourites' menu and a three-for-a-fiver bottled beer offer, has instead acquired cult status due to its positioning on the corner between The Arches and The Sub Club. On busy nights the queues to each will scrawl down and meet outside this very establishment. Accordingly clientele ranges from thirsty shoppers during the day to beautiful young things and technoheads come party-time, a monitoring the queue situation from the window. And they sell Jupiler on tap

🍺 *Mon–Sun, 10am–12pm;*
Food, Mon–Sun, 10am–10pm

The Doublet

74 Park Road

(0141) 334 1982

A bohemian little character with many a story to tell, just round from Woodlands Road and the university. But not bohemian enough to insist that you wear doublets to get in, unfortunately. Upon entrance you'd think that you'd entered a private party such is the level of homeliness and the way that everyone seems to be everyone else's best mate. Rock band Biffy Clyro took Zane Lowe here when he was interviewing them for Gonzo. Also about the only place where you can get Cruzcampo on tap.

🕒 *Mon, 11am–11pm; Tue–Sat, 11am–12pm; Sun, 12.30pm–11pm; Food, Mon–Sat, 12am–9pm; Sun, 12.30pm–9pm*

The Halt Bar

160 Woodland's Road

(0141) 352 9996

Muso-boho haunt number one. The old man staring into his pint behind you is probably a breathtaking jazz saxophonist; it's that sort of place. The Halt is the epitome of the eclecticism that the West End can offer, the local for a sizeable portion of the mad, brilliant people that live in the flats nearby. Heaving at the weekend, especially during and after the Saturday afternoon jam sessions. Big football pub too and the spread of genres and nights advertised on the posters all over the walls show its open minded approach to all things musical as well.

🕒 *Mon–Sat, 12pm–12am; Sun, 12.30pm–12am; Food, Mon–Thu, 12pm–8pm; Fri–Sun, 12pm–6pm*

The Horseshoe Bar

17–19 Drury Street

(0141) 229 5711

Ask a Glaswegian about the Horseshoe and you will almost certainly get one of four responses: 1) 'The longest bar in Europe,' which it is. 2) 'Stag/hen night central,' which it is also. Its sheer size and toleration of rowdiness make it ideal, you see … 3) 'Travis used to rehearse there,' which they did, in the room upstairs, as proven by the gold discs hanging proudly behind the bar. 4) 'Legendary karaoke night,' which again, is true. *Pop Idol* winner Michelle McManus cut her teeth here. Then she ate all the pies.

🕒 *Mon–Sat, 11am–12am; Sun, 12.30pm–12am; Food, Mon–Sat, 12pm–2.30pm; Sun, 12.30pm–5pm*

Drink

Jinty McGinty's
Ashton Lane
(0141) 339 0747

Ignore the comically rhyming name (unless you're looking for a way to irritate your mates, in which case repeating it over and over again is a pretty good way of doing so), this is a proper Irish pub with some of Ireland's favourite literary sons adorning the walls and some of its favourite meals appearing in the menu. Celtic music is the soundtrack, often live, and in the evenings customers will spill out onto Ashton Lane and engage in the general merriness which sees Jinty's consistently named as one of Glasgow's favourite watering holes.

🍺 Mon–Sat, 11am–12am, Sun, 12.30pm–12am; Food, Mon–Thu, 12pm–3pm, Fri & Sat, 12pm–4pm, Sun, 12.30pm–3pm

MacSorley's
42 Jamaica Street
(0141) 248 8581

Walking by this live music venue it's a reasonable bet you'll hear 'Mustang Sally' getting churned out by yet another pub band. That's not to knock MacSorley's – which does exactly what it sets out to and puts on that certain type of foot-stomping rock for that certain type of beer-drinking fella. You can be sure that conversations about 'the classics' here are inevitably going to involve at least one mention of Brown-eyed Girl, but if you're lucky you'll also occasionally catch some younger bands actually doing their own material.

🍺 Mon–Sat, 12pm–12am; Sun, 12.30pm–1am

Nice'n'Sleazy
421 Sauchiehall Street, City Centre
(0141) 333 0900

Don't be put off by the naff student flat décor – Sleazy's is one of Glasgow's coolest hangouts for indie kids and music lovers. The walls leading downstairs to the gig venue are lined with posters for local gigs of all sorts, and Monday's open-mic night is almost as much of an institution as the pub itself. Snow Patrol used to hang out here, Aidan Moffat from Arab Strap DJs on Saturdays and John Peel said the jukebox was 'the best in Britain'. Best of all, they do carryout so you won't be left dry when you end up at a naff student flat partying with the indie kids.

🍺 Mon–Sat, 11.30am–12am; Sun, 12.30pm–12am; Food, Mon–Sat, 11.30am–8pm; Sun, 12.30pm–8pm

O'Henry's
14 Drury Street
(0141) 248 3751

One can tell a lot about a Glaswegian male by whether he thinks of O'Henry's as 'the pub opposite The Truffle Club' (a lapdancing bar) or conversely of the Truf as 'that place facing O'Henry's'. Although both serve alcohol it's only O'Henry's that offers an old-fashioned pub atmosphere to a younger crowd, with a basement downstairs hosting singer/songwriter and rock music nights ('Heads Down, Thumbs Up', last Saturday of the month, is the best). Plus, they let you in with trainers. Which is not the case with The Truffle Club (err.. so we're told).
◐ *Mon–Sun, 12pm–12am; Food, Mon–Wed, 12pm–5pm; Thu–Sat, 12pm–6pm*

The Scotia Bar
112 Stockwell Street
(0141) 552 8681

This place stakes a claim to be Glasgow's oldest pub, where travellers, poets and musicians are welcome. It's certainly old-fashioned and proper, with high quality residencies from acts like The Vagabonds (Thursday nights) giving it a nice feel. Whilst you can generally sense the heritage, the pool hall upstairs can occasionally attract a less-than-scrupulous looking element. So it's worth mentioning that The Scotia's tradition is not without a sense of menace at times, however.
◐ *Mon–Sat, 11am–12am; Sun, 12.30pm–12am; Food, Mon–Sat, 12pm–3pm; Sun, 12.30pm–3pm*

O'Neill's
Merchant Square, 71 Albion Street
(0141) 552 0822

Location, location, location. This branch of O'Neill's is surrounded by the swish bars we associate with Merchant Square and its presence is welcome for anyone who wants a bit of semi-authentic (Irish-ish) pub action instead. The seats in the outdoor courtyard (fret not, it's still under a roof and it's heated) tend to go quite quickly but are worth keeping an eye out for. Comfy leather couches and a formidable Tex-Mex sharing platter (told you it wasn't that authentic) are favourites as well.
◐ *Mon–Sat, 12pm–12am; Sun, 12.30pm–12am; Food, Mon–Sat, 12pm–7.30pm; Sun, 12.30pm–7.30pm*

Drink

Stereo

12–14 Kelvinhaugh Street

(0141) 576 5018

That it's the pub in the Franz Ferdinand video for 'Darts of Pleasure' might be enough for you keen art-poppers. If that's not enough, consider that many of the art school students and general indie-bohemians who live nearby consider it their local or that it's something of a pre-club indie hangout with some very crazy music to be heard. Grubby, laid-back... you get the picture; you know the type. Those who like it love it. Those who don't, probably aren't interested in this review, anyway.

🍸 *Mon–Fri, 5pm–12am; Sat & Sun, 1pm–12am; Food, Mon–Fri, 5pm–10.30pm; Sat & Sun, 1pm–10.30pm*

Uisge Beatha

232 Woodlands Road

(0141) 564 1596

Gaelic for 'water of life' or 'whisky' (which, for the sad linguists among you, is a similar derivation to that which 'wodka' has in Polish, them both being the crop of the land turned into a powerful and some would say life-giving drink. The native Americans, however, referred to whisky as 'Firewater', not only because of its fierce taste but – sorry, enough). A decent selection of whiskies is available in this classy pub, halfway between the City Centre and the hub of the West End. Always warm and welcoming, with tartan-clad staff and food which is fleetingly available but impressive.

🍸 *Mon–Sun, 12pm–12am; Food, Mon–Fri, 12pm–3pm*

Variety Bar

401 Sauchiehall Street

(0141) 332 4449

The name could easily describe the clientele: old men/arty types/serious dance music fans... a fantastic hotchpotch, you might say, or a motley crew perhaps (nothing to do with the tattooed, '80s rockers). Plus the staff are all hot (god knows what they do when training them) and pretty damn cool as well. If you're unsure where to go clubbing and you're a serious dance music fan, then go here and see what's on 'cos all the flyer teams come in to plug the various nights they've ended up promoting. This place is top-drawer, without trying at all.

🍸 *Mon–Sat, 11am–12am; Sun, 12.30pm–12am*

CHAT-UP LINES

THANKS TO ITCHY, YOU NEVER HAVE TO GO HOME ALONE. HOWEVER, PLEASE BE AWARE THAT WE TAKE NO RESPONSIBILITY FOR YOUR ACTIONS AFTERWARDS.

– 'The word of the day is "legs". Let's go back to my place and spread the word.'

– 'Your eyes are like spanners... Every time you look at me my nuts tighten.'

– Break a bit of ice on the bar and say, 'Now I've broken the ice can I buy you a drink?'

– 'You remind me of a parking ticket. Because you've got "fine" written all over you.'

– 'Are you wearing mirrored pants? (They say no.) Funny, because I can see myself in them.'

– 'Hi, I'm Mr Right. Someone said you were looking for me.'

– 'What's the name of that hot, black drink they sell in Starbucks?' (They reply, 'Coffee'). 'Sure. Your place or mine?'

– 'Will you help me find my lost puppy? I think he just went into a cheap hotel room over the road.'

– 'Do you like animals? Because I'm a real wildcat when you get to know me.'

– 'Have you just farted? Because you've blown me away.'

– 'I'm no Fred Flintstone, but I can sure make your bed rock.'

– 'Shag me if I'm wrong, but haven't we met before?'

– 'Do you play the trumpet? Only you're making me horny.'

Illustration by Ben Anderson–Bauer

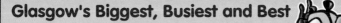

Dance

Dance

CLUBS

The Arches
30 Midland Street
(0141) 565 1000

The daddy of the Glasgow club scene. More popular than Pete Doherty in a drugs den on payday, this little gem attracts people from all walks of life with the same thing in mind – to dance until their feet fall off. Fill your greedy little clubbing ears full of serious tunes that will make you throw shapes until the wee small hours. Attracting DJs from all over the universe, this place means business and judging by the queues of eager faces outside, they do too.

Thu–Sun, 11pm–3am

£5–£22, depending on event

Art School
167 Renfrew Street
(0141) 353 4530

Possibly the hippest student venue in the whole wide world. Cheap booze is always a winner, but the atmosphere here is the main reason to grab a passing student and get yourself signed in. Forget the geeky 'student' image, this place is teeming with hotties who can actually hold a conversation without including the phrase 'awright doll/big man' and won't glare at newcomers in a menacing manner. There's a varied mix of music and the dance nights are legendary with some of the best DJs around doing their thang. Oh, and Franz Ferdinand started out here.

10pm–1am

Prices vary

Bamboo
51 West Regent Street
(0141) 332 1067

Smoother than James Bond covered in chocolate, Bamboo will charm the pants off you, get you drunk (more so on Wednesdays when all drinks are only a quid), play your favourite tunes then leave you squirming in anticipation, wondering when you'll be able to do it all again. And if you dress up in your best clobber you might even find your mug plastered all over its website for the whole world to see. Keep your peepers peeled for the Itchy crew in various states of disarray. We regularly rock up for a spot of debauchery.
© *Sat–Thu, 8pm–3am; Fri, 5pm–3am*
€ *£3–8*

The Cathouse
15 Union Street
(0141) 248 6606

Leave your Burberry at the door, dust off your coffin and get ready to dance your Nu Rock boots off. When old and new metal charge at each other like raging bulls, the result is bleedin' electric. With a sound system designed to wake the dead, more vamps in black than you can shake a stick at and a feel-good vibe that will have you grinning and dancing like a maniac, this place is a rawwk paradise. If loud, dark and uninhibited is your bag, then don your goth glad rags and look no further.
© *Thu–Sun, 11pm–3am;
Fri–Sat, 10.30pm–3am*
€ *£3–5*

Dance

Club v dub

165 Hope Street
(0141) 248 2004

Leave the camper van at home. A recent addition to Glasgow's ever-expanding city centre. Reasonably priced drinks, tunes you can bop yer head along to and a decent elevated seating area where you can chat and spot your next conquest on the dancefloor. The atmosphere is always friendly and inviting, but bear in mind that this place gets rammed at the weekend. Every Saturday DJ Big Country from Vodka Wodka plays funky house, R'n'B and classic choon anthems. Make sure you bob onto their website to get hold of flyers for club night discounts.

Mon–Sat, 11.30pm–3am
Prices vary

Cube

32–34 Queen Street
(0141) 226 8990

Renowned around Glasgow for its brilliant R'n'B nights, Cube is fast becoming the choice clubbing venue for folk who dream of being an extra in *Footballers' Wives* one day. The Club itself is pretty stylish and the music varies from night to night, as do the decent drinks promos. The only drawback is that its popularity is unfortunately reflected in the lines of bright-eyed hopefuls stretching down Queen Street but if you've got the patience (and the shoes) then Cube comes up with the goods.

Thu–Sat, 5pm-3am;
Sun–Wed, 11pm-3am
£2–3

Fury Murry's
96 Maxwell Street
(0141) 221 6511

If it's cheap drinks you're after, this place has got 'em in spades. But if you want to indulge, then make sure you get here early, as it's often packed to the rafters with punters unashamedly busting some lunatic moves to the cracking soundtrack of student classics. Which is odd, considering the average age of the clientele come the weekend would at best qualify them as mature students. Round up your old uni mates, get nicely tanked up and head on down for the nocturnal equivalent of an alcoholic Friends Reunited. Nice.

🕐 *Thu-Sat, 10.30pm-3am*
💷 *£4*

The Garage
490 Sauchiehall Street
(0141) 332 1120

What it lacks in the looks department, the Garage more than makes up for with personality. This place will soon have you falling head over heels in love and not caring that it's a bit rough round the edges. Many happy students mingle with pop lovers, rockers and dance dudes, creating a big smiley drunken mess that never fails to delight. If you secretly (or maybe not so secretly) love both Steps and Oasis, you can dance until the early hours safe in the knowledge that the only thing to hit you will be the aftershock you necked earlier.

🕐 *Mon–Sun, 11pm–3am; Fri, 10.30pm–3am*
💷 *Prices vary*

Dance

Queen Margaret University Union

22 University Gardens, Glasgow University

(0141) 339 9784

Famed for intimate gigs from bands like the White Stripes and the Chilli Peppers, the QMU is student nightlife at its best. The popular club nights host everything from pop to rock, dance and even an open-mic night. Jim's Bar and Qudos hold regular events from live bands to quiz nights. Despite the royal name, there is nothing stuffy or ladylike about this place; this is where the studying stops and the partying begins. This place has hectic dancing shoes and its not afraid to use them.

Mon–Fri, 11am–2am;

Sat–Sun, 6.30pm–2am

Prices vary

Sub Club

22 Jamaica Street

(0141) 248 4600

This place is a Glasgow institution, which is frequented by die-hard fans and newcomers alike. It's an underground club that bangs out tunes so hardcore they'll make your teeth rattle. It's currently favoured by students, neds, tarts, vicars and pretty much anyone who feels the need to raise their hands to the ceiling and dance like their life depended on it. The club itself isn't the most welcoming place in town, but if you're hard enough to venture in, then you won't be too pushed about the overwhelming lack of coasters, serviettes or little fluffy pillows.

Wed–Sun, 11pm–3am

Prices vary

CATHOUSE BORN 1990

ROCK · METAL · '80s · BLUES · ALT · ELECTRO · 6 NIGHTS A WEEK

TUE ROCK KARAOKE
Live on Stage 1

WED GAIN
Metal / Industrial

THU SKINT
Mish Mash Mayhem

FRI BALLBREAKER / VICE
You can't handle the rock

SAT SATURDAYS
The Alternative Weekend

SUN SPANK
Rock & Punk Requests

The original trademark of a Rock 'n' Roll lifestyle!

15 UNION STREET, GLASGOW. WWW.CATHOUSE.GLASGOW.CO.UK

GET INTO THE GROOVE

'I BET THAT YOU LOOK GOOD ON THE DANCEFLOOR', SING THE ARCTIC MONKEYS.
JUDGING BY THE SHAMBOLIC MOVES ON MOST CITY CENTRE DANCEFLOORS,
THEY LOST THAT BET. FOLLOW THE GUIDE TO SHAKIN' YOUR ASS LIKE ITCHY, AND
PREPARE TO BE THE TALK OF THE TOWN (FOR ALL THE RIGHT REASONS).

Illustration by Anja Wohlstrom

1.

1. **The Travolta**
   Reach for the sky and reclaim
   this classic from yer dad.
2. **Hand spin**
   Twirl those legs like a castrato.
3. **Step and clap**
   This simple move served Rick
   Astley well in the 80s, so nick
   it for the noughties.

2.

3.

Gay

Gay

BARS

Delmonicas
68 Virginia Street
(0141) 552 4803

A long-running and immensely popular bar. This place is as central as you can get for a gay venue in Glasgow; right beside the Polo and near Bennett's. It's quite classy (the G1 Group own it, which helps), but is unashamedly rowdy at night and unapologetically cheesy in its choice of tunes. Go on a Sunday (when the legendary karaoke takes place) and you can sing along to the poptastic soundtrack. The only downside (apart from your bum notes on *Angels*) is that they don't serve food.

Mon–Sun, 12pm–12am

£9

Revolver Bar
6a John Street
(0141) 553 2456

Unassuming bar that lets its music do the talking – seven and half thousand songs on the jukebox, all of which are free. All ages, shapes and sizes pop in, often before heading round the corner to one of the clubs. If you're not going out afterwards, you might check out the nearby 'gay chippy' (how fabulously witty... which silver tongued genius came up with that nickname?). Their smoked sausage and steak pie suppers are both damn tasty. Well worth a visit, if you can bear to hear the inevitable 'hilarious' jokes about smoking sausages, that is. Ooo-err, missus.

Mon–Fri, 12pm–12am; Sat–Sun, 1pm–12am

PUBS

The Waterloo
306 Waterloo Street
(0141) 229 5890

Its location on the 'wrong' side of the Hielanman's Umbrella (that's the point where the railway crosses over Argyle Street, folks: so called because after the highland clearances, the newly arrived and homeless hielanman would be forced to take shelter here when it rained) doesn't stop The Waterloo drawing quite a few middle-aged men, most nights of the week. This place is a peculiar balance of restraint and flamboyance, but it sure does a damn good pint. Which is pretty much all that matters, eh?

Mon–Sat, 12pm–12am; Sun, 12.30pm–12am

CLUBS

Bennets

80–90 Glassford Street

(0141) 552 5761

The seedier side of Glasgow's upbeat gay scene. You either love it or absolutely hate it and the latter seems to be the majority. The bouncers seem to let any old punter in: dirty old men, neds, almost like a gay version of Destiny. The club itself, even though recently refurbished, is grotty to say the least. You can see PAs here from unknown bands who must leave in a shaken state. If that doesn't grab your attention randy punters will whip off their t-shirts and recreate something from a nightmare.

Ⓒ *Wed–Sun, 11.30pm–3.30am*

Ⓔ *Prices vary*

Utter Gutter @ The Riverside Club

33 Fox Street

(0141) 248 3144

Glasgow's coolest night for gay, straight, bi and fabulous peeps, which has been growing rapidly and seen guest slots from the likes of Lady Miss Kier. Housed, oddly, in a venue usually used for ceilidhs, it's frequented by beautiful boys in spandex T-shirts, glam girls in catsuits and everything else in between (there's a mental image for you). Madame Sannex and Hushpuppy keep the crowds shakin' it till the early hours, playing a cutting edge mix of electronica, pure pop, house, funk, disco and rock.

Ⓒ *Last Fri of the month, 12am–3am*

Ⓔ *£10*

Gay

SHOPS

Clone Zone
45 Virginia Street
(0141) 553 2666
Part of a national chain specialising in gay mens' gear, from outfits to DVDs.
🕐 *Mon–Sat, 10.30am–7pm;*
Sun, 12.30pm–6pm

Joys-4-Us
11 Dixon Street
(0141) 248 6064
Underwear and books are among the more discreet products on offer in this full-tilt store housed in the LGBT centre. Treat yourself right nice with a purple double-ender and a butt plug.
🕐 *Mon–Fri, 9am–4pm*

OTHER

Glasgow LGBT
11 Dixon Street
(0141) 221 7203
Your first stop for info about gay life in Glasgow, housing a café bar, a legal surgery, shop, youth groups and health projects.
🕐 *Mon–Sun, 11am–12am*

Glasgow Uni LGBT
John McIntyre Building, University Avenue
(0141) 339 8697
If you're a student at Glasgow, who needs support, advice, or just wants to meet up with other like-minded people at events, then this society is quite possibly the place for you.
🕐 *Mon–Sun, 11am–12am*

LISTEN UP
OMI PALONES!

THOSE OF YOU OUT CHARPERING FOR A DOLLY DISH WITH A NICE BASKET MIGHT WANT TO TAKE NOTE OF AN IMMINENT LINGUISTIC REVIVAL ON THE UK GAY SCENE.

Polari, the secret language used by London's 1960s gay community to communicate in public without fear of the law, has long been as dead as a dodo's cassette collection.

But the pink parlance is starting to come back out of the closet. What with a reinvigorated Morrissey being a self-confessed polari user, as well as usage of polari becoming almost compulsory amongst staff at popular London kitsch cabaret venue Madame JoJo's, it looks like pretty soon anyone who's anyone will need to know their fantabuloso lingo.

I'M BONAR FOR THAT OMI PALONE

'What a cod meese omi'
– 'What a vile ugly man'

'Vada the colour of his eyes'
- 'Check out the size of his penis'

'Vada the palone with the matini'
- 'Look, he's gay'

'I'm bonar for that omi palone'
- 'I'm attracted to that man'

'Nice basket'
- 'Nice trouser bulge'

'You're joshed up'
– 'You're looking your best'

'Aunt Nell!'
– 'Listen to me!'

'Vada the cod zhoosh on that omi palone'
– 'Look at the awful clothes on that man'

'Nanti vogue near me'
– 'Don't light that cigarette near me'

'Let's blag some dishes'
– 'Let's pick up some good-looking guys'

'There's nix mungarlee here'
– 'There's nothing to eat here'

Shopping

Shop

AREAS

Buchanan Street

Home to Princes Square, the jewellers' paradise of Argyle Arcade, Frasers, Diesel and Lush, Buchanan Street is Glasgow's 'choice' shopping district. Stores like Game and Forbidden Planet cater for the geeks. A better experience than Argyle Street.

Merchant City

For the dedicated follower of fashion, this is a wet dream. Home to all things pretentious and trendy, If you've just been paid, or if celeb-spotting is your bag, try here, although you're more likely to see anonymous posh babes vacantly fighting over Versace handbags than David Beckham choosing some designer pants.

Sauchiehall Street

Longer than a stretch in prison, Sauchiehall Street, once famed for its quality shops and tearooms, is now slightly old hat, drawing crowds of school children and teenagers rather than hardcore shoppers. Ann Summers, BHS and River Island all live here, but it's not the shoppers' paradise it once was.

West End

If the sight of another chain store makes you want to rip your own arm off, then run quickly waving your arms wildly toward the west end. Students, well off couples and trendy folk flock here to soak up the bohemian, chic, individual and sometimes pricey shops lounging casually next to trendy pubs and restaurants.

MARKETS

The Barras

Glasgow Cross
(0141) 552 4601

There's a guy selling towels and he's not asking a tenner, he's not asking a fiver; he's not even asking for a quid. He's asking you not to grass him up to the cops, cos his goods are knocked off. Mind you, we're sure some of the stuff here has come out of the right end of a lorry. Love it or hate it, the Barras is about as Glaswegian as it gets. This place has been here for donkey's years and properly captures the traditional spirit of Glas'gae. The ideal place to buy 50lbs of meat, 20 tea towels or a gas lighter.

⏱ *Sat–Sun, 10am–5pm*

DEPARTMENT STORES

Frasers
Buchanan Street
(0141) 221 3880

Frasers is a great big monster of a department store all wrapped up in a delicate, shiny little package. You'll find this beauty of a shop sitting at the bottom of Buchanan Street, and you can spend the whole day here buying everything from perfume to cutlery, lipstick to designer suits. It looks nice, smells great, has everything you could ever want or need and if it wasn't a building you'd probably marry it. Assuming it said yes, that is. It must get a lot of offers.

Mon–Wed, Fri–Sat, 9am–6pm; Thu, 9.30am–8pm; Sun, 12pm–5.30pm

MENS' CLOTHING

Hugo Boss
55–79 Buchanan Street
(0141) 221 7168

Perhaps the first standalone designer-boutique to open in Glasgow after its 'relaunch' following its year as European City of Culture in 1990. The German label has quietly and methodically done a brilliant trade in a way so very appropriate for both the nationality of the store, and the understated suits (upstairs) and casualwear (ground floor) on offer. One of the few places to actually stock 34" jackets, and has a range of jolly good sale prices too.

Mon–Wed & Fri–Sat, 9.30am–6pm; Thu, 9.30am–7pm; Sun, 12pm–5pm

John Lewis
Buchanan Street
(0141) 353 6677

'Never knowlingly undersold.' Gotta love such a sneaky tag-line. Good old John Lewis. It's about as risqué as a pair of support tights. They stock everything a department store should, and aren't afraid to charge a little more for quality. This sets the produce here above the usual fare. You can wander around in a nice setting, get a cappuccino and then buy something 'well made' for your mum because, 'You can't go wrong with John Lewis, you know'. Probably best not to buy her a pair of those support tights, though.

Mon–Tue, Fri–Sat, 9am–6pm; Wed, 9.30am–6pm; Thu, 9am–8pm; Sun, 11am–5pm

Slater Menswear
165 Howard Street
(0141) 552 7171

Slater Menswear is a gigantic, nine floor, one-stop-shop for all tailoring needs. The biggest menswear store in the world, no less. Staff are abundant and nifty with measuring tapes to get you suited and booted in no time. State your case: 'wedding … three days … pinstripe … navy … make me look two-stone lighter' (steady) and let them do the rest. Most Glasgow males have procured a whistle'n'flute from Slater's – it just sort of happens one day. There's a designer room, an adjustment service, formalwear and kilt hire, too.

Mon–Wed, Fri & Sat 8.30am–5.30pm; Thu, 8.30am–7.30pm; Sun, 11.30am–4.30pm

Shop

UNISEX CLOTHING

Cruise
180–188 & 223 Ingram Street
(0141) 572 3232

Every city has a store with a bag that everyone wants, and Cruise's gigantic black number is Glasgow's. You'll see them around town on a Saturday, perhaps containing a Prada dress, or something a bit more funky from the store which focuses on diffusion lines and streetwear. Some seriously cool limited-edition trainers and t-shirts can be found in the Oki-Ni section up the back. Don't be intimidated by the fact you need to buzz in – it's not up its own arse at all. Go on, ring that bell, rock star...

Mon–Wed & Fri, 10am–6pm; Thu, 10am–7pm; Sat, 9.30am–6pm; Sun, 12pm–5pm

WOMENS' CLOTHING

Big Ideas
9 Ingram Street
(0141) 552 2722

Big Ideas does designer gear for size 16s and over... a breath of fresh air for those who want a special outfit but can't face the baggy sacks and multi-coloured tents of other plus-size stores. This place understands that tailored outfits which fit are actually more flattering than attempting to wear a loose kaftan as it that disguises something. Long coats, trouser suits, skirts and jumpers all line the shelves in decent materials. It might be pricey, but hey, this is the Italian Centre, so what did you expect?

Mon–Sat, 9.30am–5.30pm

Zara
10–16 Buchanan Street
(0141) 227 4770

Since it opened in 2004, Spanish cothing giant Zara's European-city-chic has gone down well in cosmopolitan Glasgow. The womenswear can be flouncy, flowing or tailored but it's always defined by its brisk Spanish stylings. Mind you, we've yet to find any laydee who can wear their trousers without turning them up or wearing 6-inch killer heels. Maybe they're all giants in Spain. Menswear has a similar ethos, offering details and finishes not often seen in high street stores, while the Zara jeans range is incredibly well-priced for the quality.

Mon–Wed, Fri & Sat, 9.30am–6pm; Thu, 9.30am–8pm; Sun, 11am–5pm

H&M
Buchanan Galleries
(0141) 352 6980

Totally bargainsville. Masses of cheap-as-chips, here today gone tomorrow fashion you'll wear every Saturday night for a month then dump – which is fine, at these prices. The main drawback is the fact it's almost always mobbed. It can be hard to find anything as people randomly seem to chuck things about on the floor after rifling through the racks. Also, we hear the changing rooms are a bit messy – the massive queues have always put us off having an actual look. But if you're not afraid to try on gear in the midst of a crowd of fashion-crazed shoppers, this could be for you.

Mon–Wed & Fri-Sat, 9am–6pm; Thu, 9am–8pm; Sun, 11am–5pm

SECONDHAND

Cancer Research UK

269 Sauchiehall Street
(0141) 332 8204

As with any city, Glasgow has ample charity stores, including about ten in the Byres Road/Great Western Road area alone. This one in the city centre stands out, however, because of the inordinately high number of designer items in great condition. We reckon that the stock is moved here from other outlets. Either that, or there's a group of extremely generous fashionistas who live very close to it. Certainly, finds like Armani shoes, Liberty scarves and Jaeger shirts make it well worth a peek.

Mon–Sat, 9am–5pm

SHOES

Schuh

112 Argyle Street
(0141) 248 7331

From magic slippers to big tough kickers, Schuh has plenty to click your heels about, with quirky designs and loud colours for you to strut your funky stuff down the streets of Glasgow. These shoes make modern art look tame. Quality can be cruel to your credit card but a student discount makes this all so guilt free. Well, under 20 per cent guilt free anyway. This place is stomping. As will be your friends when they see how much cooler your shoes are than theirs.

Mon–Sat, 9am–6.30pm; Thu, 9am–7.30pm; Sun, 11am–5.30pm

Glory Hole

Ruthven Lane
(0141) 357 5662

Erm, not exactly the kind of name we'd choose for a store. Unless we wanted the place to be rammed with the dirty mac brigade, that is. Still, in a way this is quite an appropriately named place – hidden in a wee arcade behind Ruthven Lane, with many treasures to be discovered. Recent styles and labels of a standard 'thrift store' spread are joined by vintage jewellery and shoes, and some gorgeous scarves. And, fortunately the city's doggers have yet to get wind of the name, so you can still go and browse the range of nice apparel without some perv exposing himself to you. Which is always nice.

Mon–Sat, 11am–5.30pm; Sun, 1pm–5pm

Shop

BOOKS

Caledonia Books
483 Great Western Road
(0141) 334 9663

Ahhh, a good old fashioned bygone bookshop. The walls are crammed from top to bottom with a treasure chest of well-loved and ancient novels and texts. This is a grotto for many rare editions – really jammy folks can even get their mitts on the odd signed copy. Amazingly, most of the books in here are only slightly more expensive than the price of your average second hand read. As the late, great Freddie Mercury once sang, 'It's a kind of magic'. He was probably singing about this place.
🕒 *Mon–Sat, 10.30am–6pm*

Voltaire & Rousseau
12–14 Otago Lane
(0141) 339 1811

Voltaire and Rousseau is a quaint nest of second hand books. Like birds flapping over their prized eggs, the staff are knowledgeable, warm and welcoming. Which is how we imagine birds flapping over their eggs to be. Well, owls at least. They're wise aren't they? Ahem, anyway, get yourself in here and delve into the gold mine of obscure books; history buffins in particular will have a field day. Be prepared to spend some serious time rooting and exploring for exactly what you want, but it's worth it. The books are cheap as chips and you'll fly away a happy little chick. Awww.
🕒 *Mon–Sat, 10am–6.30pm*

Ottakar's
Buchanan Galleries, 220 Buchanan Street
(0141) 353 1500

If your granny emptied her attic and put all her unread books into a shop, it would look like Ottakar's: slightly dated, but cosy and comfortable. Although quite how your granny would have got hold of all the latest major releases in pretty much every category you could hope for, is a question that needs explaining. In between shelves, there's the odd little gem: alternative contemporary fiction that didn't get shelf space in bigger book chains. And there's a cushy little coffee shop to rest your weary feet and let your credit card get its breath back. A veritable home from home.
🕒 *Mon–Sat, 9am–6pm; Thu, 9am–8pm; Sun, 11am–5pm*

Waterstone's
153–157 Sauchiehall Street
(0141) 332 9105

A bookworm's wildest fantasy. From fact to fiction and poetry to plays, there are masses of books to keep the reading junkie in a page turning frenzy. If it ain't on these shelves, then it's not worth the eyestrain. But this is no ordinary shop. Early evening book groups have made reading the sexiest, smartest and sophisticated way to play the dating game. From now on, during the first part of the evening, the location of this branch of Waterstone's is less Sauchiehall Street than it is Saucey-hall street. Get ye down there, singletons.
🕒 *Mon–Fri, 8.30am–9pm; Sat, 9am–8pm; Sun, 10.30am–7pm*

MUSIC

Avalanche Records

34 Dundas Street

(0141) 332 2099

If all the cheese in pop music is starting to go mouldy, and you don't really have the taste for Stilton, you want to get a taste of this place. Retro alternative records sit among underground sub-culture tracks, and for the hardcore music guru there's always something new to tune your ears into. You can even take a walk on the wild side and pick up an album on vinyl – the crackle adds to the nostalgia, apparently, and it's just the warmest way to listen to tunes, man. You'll never eat cheese again.

Ⓒ *Mon–Sat, 9.30am–6pm; Thu, 9.30am–7pm; Sun, 12pm–6pm*

Fopp

358 Byres Road

(0141) 357 0774

Nothing to do with floppy-haired Hugh Grant-a-likes, this place is a beguiling little cavern of musical treats. For some, visiting Fopp is a hobby, a place to chill-out and be seen. From retro to hip-hop, it sells music for the hardcore enthusiast that's not going to cost you an arm and a leg. There's masses of stuff at £5 and £10. Throw in a few current chart tunes, classic DVDs and books of oddity and you get one of the most unashamedly trendy joints in Glasgow. So all you side-parted, 'gosh' merchants should find somewhere else to talk about your pashed-up love of *Four Weddings*.

Ⓒ *Mon–Sat, 9.30am–7pm; Sun, 11am–6pm*

Music Zone

54 Sauchiehall Street

(0141) 353 6250

Judging by the big butch bouncer on the door, the music in here should be gold-plated. Instead, the excessive security is probably due to shoplifting neds. Once you have overcome the eyes of interrogation as you walk through the door, Music Zone is one lucky find. Cheap, no-frills chart tunes to bump up your collection, as well as a good range of the cheapest DVDs you're likely to find this side of the dodgy characters hanging around late-night pubs offering you discs featuring footage of people getting up half-way through the film to go for a piss.

Ⓒ *Mon–Sat, 9am–6.30pm; Thu, 9am–7pm; Sun, 11am–5pm*

Shop

OTHER

Grassroots Organic Food Shop
20 Woodlands Road
(0141) 353 3278

The vegetarian's paradise, though it's also great for anyone who wants to eat organic, buy cruelty-free products or who just prefers to shop locally and cook rather than stock up on cardboardy ready meals from a supermarket. This place has got heaps of veg, soya and tofu, beans, pulses, the Ecover range, fresh herbs, healthy takeaways and much more. They also host occasional food and health-related events here too.

🕔 *Mon–Wed, 8am–6pm; Thu–Fri, 8am–7pm; Sat, 9am–6pm; Sun, 11am–5pm*

Lupe Go Lightly
520 Great Western Road
(0141) 334 6003

If Lupe was a person, she'd be a crazy girl with punk on her MP3 player, half-a-dozen plastic rings on her fingers and pop art posters all over her walls. Instead, Lupe is a tiny and funky shop, which sells unique products by local designers. They range from the collectible and pricey to the cheap and fun, but all with an alternative, anti-fashion, pro-music style. Lupe Go Lightly is a great place for cards, earrings, cushions and unusual ornaments, as well as some snazzy tops. But nothing to do with crazy, punk-loving, plastic-ringed, young ladies with an interest in pop art.

🕔 *Mon–Sun, 10am–6pm*

The Sentry Box
175 Great George Street
(0141) 334 6070

If you don't have any nieces or nephews, invent some quick, because otherwise everyone will know that you're playing with all these great toys just for yourself. A million miles away from the dreary plastic rubbish'r'us chainstores, this fun shop has loads of traditional games and toys, from Fuzzy Felt to Plasticine, robots to kiddy stickers, which will have you reverting to childhood in minutes and pulling the pigtails of the nearest girl to you. It's also a fun source of silly presents whether they are for actual children or just for your childish mates.

🕔 *Mon–Sat, 9.30am–5.30pm; Sun, 1pm–5pm*

AUSTIN FLOWERS
020 7697 9824

Philglas & Swiggot

R.SOLES

Spex in the City

FISHCOTHEQUE
TRADITIONAL BRITISH FISH & CHIPS
60 Seats Restaurant
Cafe Restaurant & Takeaway
Coach Orders Welcome

That's SHOE Business

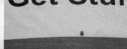

Get Stuffed

Send your favourite puntastic shop names and pics to: editor@itchymedia.co.uk

Itchy

CALLING ALL ASPIRING SNAPPERS...

We need hawk-eye photographers to contribute their sparkling talents to the Itchy City magazine.

We want the inside track on the bars, pubs, clubs and restaurants in your city, as well as bright, dynamic pictures to represent the comedy, art, music, theatre, cinema and sport scenes in your city.

If you're interested in getting involved, please send examples of your cracking photography to: editor@itchymedia.co.uk, clearly stating which city you can work in. All work will be fully credited.

Bath/Birmingham/Brighton/Bristol/Cardiff/Edinburgh/Glasgow/
Leeds/Liverpool/London/Manchester/Nottingham/
Oxford/Sheffield/York

Out & About

Out & About

CINEMAS

Glasgow Film Theatre

12 Rose Street
(0141) 332 8128

Who better to tell us about the Glasgow Film Theatre than Obi-Wan Kenobi himself? 'GFT is a frontline player promoting the Scottish movie talent of tomorrow, bringing back the big classics of yesterday, screening the best of independent movie making from around the world and pioneering film education for all.' Cheers Ewan, but you forgot to mention that this art deco landmark has attracted everyone from school kids to Quentin Tarantino. it also has a café as cool as its clientele.

🎬 *Box Office, Mon–Sun, 12pm–9pm*
🎫 *Prices vary*

Grosvenor Cinema

24 Ashton Lane
(0141) 339 8444

Ashton Lane is the wonderland of the West End, lined with cobbles and trimmed with fairy lights, and this treasure trove of pretty-yet-trendy bars and eateries would be incomplete without the Grosvenor. Screening all the major releases with the odd classic and indie flick, the two retro-style film theatres are accompanied by as many bars as well as a restaurant. As for the best bit – the whole place is fully licensed so sipping vodka cranberrys while you lounge on the plush leather couches at the back is a must. Cinema how God intended it.

🎬 *Mon–Sun, 10am–late*
🎫 *Prices vary*

COMEDY

The Stand Comedy Club

333 Woodlands Rd
(0870) 600 6055

When the owners of the Edinburgh Stand realised they were onto a good thing, they knew it would be rude to deprive us of a western counterpart. With a cosy cabaret-inspired layout, The Stand crams big groups round tiny tables (get there early if you want a seat) meaning it has a pleasantly relaxed vibe. Staging homegrown talent as well as the big fish of the comedy pond, it attracts many a skint student with its affordable prices despite claiming to 'cater for the 25-55 year old section of the population'.

🎬 *Mon–Sun, 7.30pm–late*
🎫 *£2–£10*

THEATRE

Citizen's Theatre
119 Gorbals Street
(0141) 429 0022

Set up as the 'alternative' people's theatre, the Citizen's is now regarded as one of the leading theatres in Scotland. The likes of Rupert Everett, Glenda Jackson and the stage version of *Trainspotting* have appeared here. The main room does a steady line in adaptations of classics, while the two wee studio spaces house more experimental work, where you can see every pore on the actors' skins, if you're really interested in that kinda thang.

☺ Doors, 7.30pm
🎫 £10–£12; Conc from £4, with some free preview tickets available

Tron Theatre
63 Trongate
(0141) 552 4267

Sadly, the name of this place has nothing to do with the classic 80s cyber film, so don't turn up in your BacoFoil body-suit. However, there's a fab bar, a good restaurant… oh, and a pretty good theatre too. The Tron puts on some of the liveliest contemporary plays as well as a selection of comedy and absolutely brilliant alternative pantos which do a mad update on fairy tales, usually put together by Forbes Masson (formerly Alan Cumming's comedy partner and once played a part in EastEnders). So if you really can't resist the BacoFoil, you could at least pretend you were an extra.

☺ Doors usually 7pm
🎫 £11

Tramway
25 Albert Drive
(0141) 422 2023

A wee bit out of the way, but only five minutes on the train from Central Station, Tramway (as in it used to be a tram station) is Glasgow's most self-consciously arty theatre. The largest space here is a big empty shed, which is little changed from the tram days, where they stage experimental dramas and performance theatre, along with the odd more conventional play. Ok, maybe that's a bit of a difference from the tram days. There are also exhibition spaces upstairs, a bar/café and an unusual garden out the back.

☺ Tue–Sat, 12pm–8pm; Sun, 12pm–6pm
🎫 £6–£10

Out & About

GALLERIES

CCA

350 Sauchiehall Street
(0141) 352 4900

'I don't like cricket, I love it...'. These guys sure know how to make a lazy Sunday reggae-tinged tune. And have you heard the remix with *Independent Woman*? Brilliant. Oh no, hang on. That was *10cc* wasn't it? Oh well, there are still some rather fabulous bars and a cafe here, as well as some often experimental, usually amusing, exhibitions. Shows the Becks Futures stuff, as well as performance art and a little art house cinema. None of them are *Dreadlock Holiday*, mind you.

⏰ *Tue–Fri, 9am–10pm; Sat, 10am–10pm*
🎫 *Free*

Gallery of Modern Art

Royal Exchange Square
(0141) 229 1996

GOMA is one of the coolest galleries around and not only that, there's a brilliant library/café downstairs too. There's lots of interesting modern art but the most memorable feature is the statue of Wellington outside which has a traffic cone permanently placed a'top his head – so famous, they sell postcards of it now. Without it, Christ only knows what the student population of this city would do to make taxpayers regret their contributions to higher education. Crack, probably. Sheesh. You know what these kids are like.

⏰ *Mon–Thu & Sat, 10am–5pm;*
Fri & Sun, 11am–5pm
🎫 *Free*

The Lighthouse

11 Mitchell Lane
(0141) 225 8414

Guess who designed this imposing building which opened in 1999, the year Glasgow was voted European City of Architecture? Here's a clue: C... R... Mack... The guy was good. The Lighthouse has been transformed into a very upmarket art gallery now, featuring cutting-edge exhibitions and a groovy design shop, as well as a tower giving a great view over the city. Be warned though, there are 135 steps to scale, so asthmatics and those who enjoy chuffing on the odd cancer stick might want to get some advance training in.

⏰ *Mon & Wed–Sat, 10.30am–5pm; Tue,*
11am–5pm; Sun, 12pm–5pm
🎫 *Free*

MUSEUMS

House For An Art Lover
Bellahouston Park, 10 Dumbreck Road
(0141) 353 4449

The beautiful House For An Art Lover is proof that there was so much more to Charles Rennie Mackintosh than tacky sterling silver jewellery or rose-patterned coasters. This white-walled crowning glory of the great Glasgow architect's career was designed by Mackintosh in 1901, but it wasn't 'til long after his death that his plans were brought to fruition. Its picturesque setting in Bellahouston Park also makes it a decent party location (providing your daddy's got a black Amex).
🕒 Sun–Thu, 10am–4pm; Fri–Sat, 10am–1pm
💷 £3.50

Scottish Football Museum
Hampden Park
(0141) 616 6139

A chance for Stattos and anoraks to relive the games of days gone by in 14 galleries of footy-related memorabilia. Exhibits range from the world's oldest match ticket and trophy to Diego Maradona's strip. Not that it'd fit him nowadays. Have you seen the size of that neck? Still, nice to see he didn't get away entirely scot-free with the old 'hand of God'. And they say there's no such thing as karma... Ahem, anyway, you can also tour the stadium, and test your footballing skills by attempting to score. Then you can try your luck at the local bar.
🕒 Mon–Sat, 10am–5pm; Sun, 11am–5pm
💷 Museum, £5; Stadium tour, £6

Museum Of Piping
McPhater Street
(0141) 353 0220

To say that there is a slight similarity between the noise made by someone using a lump hammer to systematically break the bones of a bag full of kittens and the skirl of the pipes is a severe understatement. Should you be one of those people who enjoy the sound of feline torture, the Museum of Piping is the place for you. Itchy recently heard that Frankie Detorri is taking lessongs. Sweet Jesus. Brimming with fascinating information about bagpiping's history, as well as the Scottish clans, this place should keep both bagpipe enthusiasts and cat haters occupied for hours.
🕒 Mon–Sun, 9am–4.30pm
💷 £3

The Tenement House
145 Buccleuch Street
(0141) 333 0183

A lady called Agnes Toward lived here for some fifty years and didn't bother to redecorate or throw anything out. Nowadays this is the kind of behaviour that warrants Kim and Aggie turning up to your house, and screwing up their sour faces in disgust, as they patronisingly explain the basics of hoovering. However, in the Victorian era they obviously had a healthy appreciation of archiving. Since Toward's death, the National Trust have run the house as a perfect example of how the Victorian gentility used to live, right down to the table being set for afternoon tea.
🕒 Mon–Sun, 1pm–5pm (1 Mar–31 Oct only)
💷 £5

Out & About

LIVE MUSIC

13th Note Café
50–60 King Street
(0141) 553 1638

So you've sampled the meat and potatoes of the Glasgow music scene, yet your palate craves something a bit fresher; aubergine cannelloni with a sprinkling of indie to be precise. Well, then you'd better hit the 13th Note Café, where you can tuck into a vegan/vegetarian entree before descending into the basement for some music-shaped dessert. Far out of the realms of student territory, the live sets range from obscure electronica to leather-clad punk. Great for a bit of variation.

☺ *Mon–Sun, 12pm–12am*

Barrowlands
244 Gallowgate
(0141) 552 4601

If St Mungo's Hall had been available for hire the night Margaret McIver tried to book it for the 1926 Barras Market workers' Christmas dance, the Glasgow music scene would undoubtedly be a far poorer place. Having proved unsuccessful, she improvised and the Barrowland Ballroom was born. Today, the charming, shabby dance hall crackles with atmosphere and regularly crams in all-standing crowds eager for music, often welcomed by a heart-felt 'We've waited a long time to play here' from the stage. Kitsch, tacky but pure magic. Itchy hearts this place.

☺ *Times vary*

King Tut's Wah Wah Hut
272a St Vincent Street
(0141) 221 5279

Back in 1993, Alan McGee knew that King Tut's was the place to check out the cream of new musical talent, so one night he went along for a cheeky peek. Despite them supporting 18 Wheeler, he ended up liking what he saw, and signed Oasis on the spot. Today, the venue and the band tower above any other in Britain in terms of reputation, yet unlike Oasis's terminally bland recent offerings, King Tut's repeatedly serves up cutting-edge music. Fantastically intimate, pre-gig grub, booze, a jam-packed jukebox, pool table... really, what more do you need on a night out?

☺ *Mon–Sat, 12pm–12am; Sun, 6pm–12am*

STAG AND HEN NIGHTS

BREAK OUT THE L-PLATES AND LOCK UP YOUR DAUGHTERS. HERE'S ITCHY'S GUIDE TO YOUR FINAL NIGHT OF FREEDOM...

Cooooo-eeeeee big boy!

The Stand
Woodlands Road
(0870) 600 6055

Sound line-ups of decent comics all itching to tell you all about your mother-in-law and how that charming and beautiful woman you're about to marry will end up just like her. Ha-ha-ha!

Powerboat River Rocket
Dunoon
(01369) 707 054

What better way to team build before the big night than to drive over to the beautiful Scottish coast, strap the gang into a speedboat and let the obliging folk of Dunoon turn their stomachs inside out?

Bucking brilliant!

Cube
Queen Street
(0141) 226 8990

Big and loud, with drinks offers and scantily clad nurses on a Sunday, Cube provides a fine venue to shake away those last hours of 'freedom' and tell all the wrong people how much you love them.

Scotkart Cambuslang
Westburn Road
(0141) 641 0222

Was it always him? The guy who crashed routinely into lamp-posts, skips and combine-harvesters? The guy who just simply could not drive? Well if so, and you're running a bit short of material for that best man's speech, take a few minutes out and book him in for an afternoon of carnage at Scotkart. Scotland's most popular karting track specialises in big bookings, so invite along the bride's 12-year-old brother and the stoner from flat three to see if you can't engineer a pile up. You'll have plenty of speech material before the day is out.

Out & About

FURTHER AFIELD

Edinburgh

If you're thinking about heading over to Auld Reekie for a day-trip, whatever you do, don't go asking any of the Glasgow locals for their opinion on whether it's a good idea or not. Like a bickering pair of siblings, Glasgow and Edinburgh's inhabitants have spent centuries locked in a bitter squabble, even though they both clearly spend as much time in each other's cities as they do their own. Pick up a copy of the Itchy guide to Edinburgh for full details or just hop on a train to Waverley Station and wander around Princes Street Gardens, the castle and the New Town, all of which are well worth a look despite what we Glaswegians think.

Loch Lomond

Loch Lomond Tourist Information
(01301) 703 260

It mightn't have all the folklore about being rammed with sinister monsters lurking below the surface, but at 24 miles by 5 miles, this famous stretch of water, which is 600ft deep at some points, is the longest freshwater lake in Britain. Which means that ol' Nessie's a bit silly really, because at her size, if you're going to do your morning 20 lengths, you'd want to be able to get a bit of speed up before having to turn around. Plus there's a grand old view. The lake's also surrounded by a selection of fine restaurants as well as some touristy shops if you're after the usual selection of holidayer-exploiting tat.

The Falkirk Wheel

Off the M80/A80
(0870) 608 2608

The world's first and only rotating boat lift, they boast. Which doesn't sound that great, but is in fact spectacular. The Falkirk Wheel is nothing short of an engineering marvel which literally lifts boats up and shifts them over between the Forth & Clyde Canal and the Union Canal (linking them up for travel between Glasgow and Edinburgh). Yeah, yeah, we know: engineering = boring. You won't be saying that after you've seen this in action though. It's properly breathtaking. As well as a visitor centre, there's a café and shop. You can even book boat trips.

📷 *Mon–Sun, 9.30am–6pm (Apr–Oct);*
Mon–Sun, 9.30pm–5pm (Nov–Mar)
🎫 *Free*

TOURIST ATTRACTIONS

Botanic Gardens

730 Great Western Road
(0141) 334 2422

On a sunny day in Glasgow, (which happens about as frequently as pigs unfurling their shiny wings and taking to the skies), this place is heaven on earth, as hundreds of people flock here to lie about in the grass, as though drawn by some huge botanic magnet. The other 364 days of the year, they shelter from the rain by looking at the exotic plants in the greenhouse, though the main Kibble Palace is currently closed for major renovations.

📷 *Mon–Sun, 7am–sunset*
🎫 *Free*

FOOTBALL

STILL HANKER FOR THE DAYS WHEN RIVAL SCOTTISH TRIBES CLASHED IN BLOODY COMBAT OVER SQUARES OF TURF? THEN COME TO GLASGOW, WHERE THE TRADITION STILL LIVES ON.

Back in 1872 four lanky Weegies stood by a football pitch and decided they wanted a team, which they named Rangers after an English rugby club that sounded cool. Years later, they crossed a new team called Celtic, founded by the kindly Brother Wilfrid to raise funds for the Glasgow's poor, and it was love at first sight.

Glasgow is home to four teams, but the most celebrated are the big two – The Old Firm. Sporting green and blue respectively, they dominate Scottish footy, and their rivalry is legend. Both teams have staggeringly devoted fan bases whose love for their team is only met by their hatred of the other.

In recent years the silverware has been shared out fairly equally, so if you can't make up your mind which one to cheer for then just walk into your nearest pub on a match day and go with the flow.

Glasgow Celtic FC

Celtic Park Stadium
Kerrydale Street
(0845) 671 1888
Tickets £22-25

Glasgow Rangers FC

Ibrox Stadium
Edgmiston Drive
(0870) 600 1972
Tickets £20-22

Itchy

WHERE CAN YOU BUY YOUR GLASS SLIPPERS, AND AVOID TURNING INTO A PUMPKIN?

MAKE EVERY NIGHT A FAIRY TALE. THE ITCHY GUIDE IS THE INSIDERS' GUIDE, TELLING YOU WHERE TO GO TO MEET PRINCE CHARMING AND HOW TO AVOID THE UGLY SISTERS IN 16 UK CITIES.

Bath, Birmingham, Brighton, Bristol, Cambridge, Cardiff, Edinburgh, Glasgow, Leeds, Liverpool, London, Manchester, Nottingham, Oxford, Sheffield, York

Laters

Drinking out

Scotland's long tradition of indulgent licensing means that most of the Glasgow's pubs and bars serve alcohol until midnight, although when an event like Celtic Connections or the West End Festival is on, some places will stay open 'til one or later. For the more insatiable alchy types, late-night action can be found at Lowdown (158 Bath Street, 0141 331 4061, Thu–Sun 'til 3am, Fri £5 and Sat £8 after 10pm), The Corinthian (191 Ingram Street, 0141 553 1101, Fri–Sat 'til 3am, Fri £6 and Sat £8 after 11pm), and Arta (13 Walls Street, 0141 552 2101, Fri–Sat 'til 3am, £7–£8 after 11pm), though it's worth noting that all three are fairly up-market places and if you arrive steaming drunk, wearing your pants as a hat they're unlikely to let you in. Alternatively, the Russian-themed Bloc (117 Bath Street, 0141 574 6066, Sat 'til 3am, free entry) is a decent venue to complete your journey into oblivion. If all else fails, some clubs offer free entry before 11pm, so flee the bar before last orders to drink in a disco 'til 3am.

Drinking in

Off-licences shut their doors at 10pm, but a fair selection of the city's pubs will do you a pert little carry-out, with a poly bag thrown in for free. If you don't fancy brokering a deal with a gruff barman then you could always try your luck at a late night corner shop – one urban custom says that if there's fruit outside then they're selling booze. Find out if it's true.

Cigarettes at 4am

If you can't get to sleep without nicotine (or you don't want to sleep) your best bet is the 24-hour Newsbox (79 Queen Street, 0141 248 9229 and 24 Renfrew Street, 0141 333 9754). Those in the West End have the 24 hour BP store (1057 Great Western Road, 0141 334 8838) or the Shell Garage (88 Woodlands Road, 0141 352 7930).

After-hours fridge stocking

Whether it's next door having a domestic or the washing machine rumbling three floors up at four in the morning, if you find yourself awake and in need of provisions, then the outlets above can sort you out, along with the 24-hour store (380 Dumbarton Road, (0141) 342 4466) and Mo's 24-hour shop (532 Sauchiehall Street, 0141 353 0022).

Food now!

Aaaaah. The greasy late night takeaway. However much you hate the drinker's sustenance on principle, it doesn't mean you'll be any less hungry for one as you totter out of a club at three o'clock on a Sunday morning. The best early hours kebab/pizza/pakora peddler is Santini's Kitchen (6 John Street, 0141 552 5151), while at the other end of the city you can dip into some dim sum 'til 4am at the ever-popular Canton Express (407 Sauchiehall Street, 0141 332 0145). If you're one of those who likes to go with what you know, then trusty old Ronald McDonald (101 Sauchiehall Street, 0141 332 6009) is open 'til 4am, serving up his wares through a hatch. Bit like a drive-thru, without the drive.

Café society

For those of you who aren't really into clogging your arteries with fat, who don't really enjoy greying lumps passed off as some kind of meat, you may wish to eat late(ish) in more civilised surroundings. In which case the chain of Beanscene cafés (19 Skirving Street, 16 Cresswell Lane, 110 Battlefield Road, 40–42 Woodlands Road, 1365 Argyle Street and 1–3 Helena Place) will provide you with a riff-raff-defying panini, veggie stew or coffee 'til 11pm. You're going to find that they won't be prepared to make you up anything fresh at that time of the evening, but there's usually a decent amount left on display by that time of evening. And even if there isn't, whatever there is will most probably be better than your average takeaway rubbish.

THE MORNING AFTER
THE NIGHT BEFORE

LATE NIGHT DRINKING'S ALL WELL AND GOOD, BUT WAKING UP THE MORNING AFTER RARELY IS. WITH A BIT OF FORETHOUGHT YOU CAN AVOID A LOT OF PAIN. SO, AS YOU'RE STAGGERING HOME AND THE LIGHT OF THAT LATE-NIGHT SHOP SWIMS INTO FOCUS, GET IN THERE AND GRAB SOME OF THE FOLLOWING ITEMS TO MAKE YOURSELF FEEL BETTER:

Fruit juice – Fruity juices contains a good measure of fructose which, helps to burn up alcohol. And it counts as a portion of fruit and veg, so you can repair some of the previous night's damage. Less healthily, you could also pick up one of any number of sugary treats such as Mars bars or sweets. The sugar in them should have the same effect.

Beans – Along with rice, grains, cereals, peas and nuts, beans have high levels of vitamin B1, which helps you to metabolise the booze. It also stabilises the nervous system, as it's a lack of B1 which often causes the shakes.

Bananas – Bananas are high in potassium, which your body loses a lot of when you're drinking. Plus they contain high levels of headache-reducing magnesium, and are also a natural antacid which'll help with the nausea.

Sports cordial – All the toilet trips you'll have made whilst drunk'll have robbed your body of all its salts, so you'll need the salts contained in sports drinks to redress the balance.

Eggs – Eggs contain cysteine which is used by the body to mop up chemicals called free radicals. A decent fry-up will usually set you straight in no time at all.

Tomatoes – Full of antioxidants and vitamins, you should feel better about 15 minutes after eating them. Tomato juice works just as well. Alternatively, add vodka for a 'hair of the dog' style Bloody Mary.

Book cut-price, last-minute accommodation with Itchy hotels.

Itchy hotels has a late booking database of over 500,000 discount hotel rooms and up to 70% off thousands of room rates in 4-star and 5-star hotels, bed and breakfasts, guesthouses, apartments and luxury accommodation in the UK, Ireland, Europe and worldwide.

www.hotels.itchycity.co.uk

or book by phone 0870 478 6317

Sleep

Sleep

EXPENSIVE ACCOMMODATION

Art House Hotel
129 Bath Street
(0141) 221 6789
There are rooms here. With beds in. Nice.
€ Double room, £125; Suite breakfasts, £7.50-£9.50

Hilton
1 William Street
(0141) 204 5555
Once Paris has finished with whichever dumb animal she's dragged round the party circuit for an hour or two before tiring of it, she puts them here. Inside you'll find kinkajous, chihuahuas and Nicole Ritchie.
€ Queen Hilton guest room, £97

Groucho St Jude's
190 Bath Street
(0141) 352 8800
You'd have thought St Jude was quite a cheery chap being a saint, wouldn't you? Oh no. Apparently he was a right grump before he got his morning coffee. Which is why the staff here are friendly at breakfast.
€ Apartment room, £120

Belhaven Hotel
15 Belhaven Terrace
(0141) 339 3222
Belhaven Hotel is situated on Belhaven terrace. Hence the name, you see. They could have called it something enticing, but the old names are the best. If we had a hotel, we'd call it 'Free mini bar'.
€ Double room, £55-£75

MID-RANGE ACCOMMODATION

The Babbity Bowster
16–18 Blackfriars Street
(0141) 552 5055
'What?' we hear you yell. 'That's a stupid name for a hotel.' No arguments here.
€ Double room, £55

Holiday Inn Express
165 West Nile Street
(0141) 331 6800
Express is like a totally 21st-century adjective, man. Think about it: Pizza Express, Stansted Express, National Express, Starlight Express, erm, actually, maybe we'll be taking that back then.
€ Double room, £56

Rab Ha's
83 Hutcheson Street
(0141) 572 0400
We reckon this might well be the dying noise made by Rab C. Nesbitt when the realisation that his stereotype of Scotsman was found funny by approximately two people, one of whom was him.
€ Double room, £75

Moat House
Congress Road (next to SECC)
(0141) 306 9988
Imagine if you were a traveller in olden-times faced with a moat. It would really get your goat. To cross it you would need a boat. In which you could float. Across the moat. In your boat. Your moat boat.
€ Twin suite, £160

CHEAP ACCOMMODATION

Adelaides

209 Bath Street
(0141) 248 4970

We'd love to tell you that this place has the weather, surf and sand of Australia. But we'd be lying through our teeth.

☻ *Double room, £50; Breakfast, £2–£6*

Alamo Guest House

46 Gray Street
(0141) 339 2395

Full of rootin', tootin' cowboys pitting their testosterone against each other in a gun-slinging competition to see who has the biggest pair of kahunas. Or maybe that's some other Alamo.

☻ *Double room, £36–£44*

Blue Sky

65 Berkeley Street
(0141) 221 1710

Ever heard the phrase 'blue sky thinking'? Well this is where it all originates from. Book a room, and see if you can figure out what all those marketing execs are on about.

☻ *Twin room, £25-£30; Includes free e-mail facilities*

Euro Hostel

318 Clyde Street
(0141) 222 2828

It's a hostel. This means that there are lots of beds in it. As well as people sleeping in them at nights. And probably during the day too, actually, given that these places are often frequented by students.

☻ *2-bed dorm room, £41.90*

Glasgow Youth Hostel

8 Park Terrace
(0870) 004 1119

It's strange that hostels so often need to call themselves youth hostels. It's hardly as if you're going to get a group of arthritic old pensioners banging on the windows to be allowed to sleep in a cramped bunk bed.

☻ *Rooms, £26–£28*

Ibis

220 West Regent Street
(0141) 225 6000

These guys were the first ever unsigned band to appear on 'Top of the Pops'. They did that annoying single 'Kandy Pop', and then dissappeared into obscurity. Oh no, wait, that was Bis. Oh well.

☻ *Rooms from £45.95; Breakfast, £4.25*

Useful info

Useful info

UNISEX HAIRDRESSERS

Cut & Dried
118 Sauchiehall Street
(0141) 332 0066

These people will take a pair of scissors, and then they'll use them to cut your hair. What more do you need to know? It is after all, fairly (ahem) cut and dried.

Fusco's Hairdressers
89 Cambridge Street
(0141) 332 6976

'Hairdresser' is a funny word, isn't it? It's not like they put any clothes on your hair. Still, it's an interesting idea. You could end up doing it for the stars, and then maybe you could put a huge smock on the monstrosity living a'top Sharon Osbourne's head.

BEAUTY SALON

Capellini
44 Jamaica Street
(0141) 221 0574

Capellini does facials, massages, manicures, pedicures, waxing etc. Basically the full range of beauty treatments for men and women. Except for the paper bag on head.

TATTOO

Terry's Tattoo Studio
23 Chisholm Studio
(0141) 552 5740

He's a dab hand with a needle is Terry Oh yeah, he'll do you a nice line in the kind of tattoo that'd have you welcomed by Hell's Angels like one of their own.

USEFUL INFORMATION

West End Cycles
16–18 Chancellor Street, Partick
(0141) 357 1344

West End Cycles is a centrally located bike hire shop, with daily hire prices starting from £10 and weekly hire from £45 (Deposit not included.)

CAR HIRE

Hertz
(0141) 248 7736

Hiring out DVDs and videos gets boring after a while doesn't it? So why not spice up your life? Hire a car or a van instead of something to watch. At Hertz, you can get yourself a motor online from £18 per day.

TAXIS

Glasgow Taxis
(0141) 429 7070

Glasgow Taxis offers the ground-breaking service of booking black taxis online or over the phone. All of their cars are wheelchair accessible (well done) and are available 24/7. Hurrah.

Glasgow Private Hire Ltd
(0141) 222 2220

Shockingly enough, Glasgow Private Hire offer private taxi hire in Glasgow, which is available over the phone. Not only is it slightly less expensive than black cab companies, but the number is easy to remember even on the most drunken night out.

BUSES

First Bus
(0141) 423 6600

These guys have bus routes in the city and surrounding areas. Most services are frequent, with well-situated stops. Get unlimited travel with a FirstDay ticket for £2.35 with a valid student ID card.

Megabus
(0173) 863 9095

Megabus is REALLY cheap and cheerful. Well, so long as you don't mind very cramped conditions, and a seat that's about as comfortable as a wooden box. A cheery student single to Edinburgh only costs £1.50. You can book online, or buy on-board before

TRAINS

First ScotRail
Caledonian Chambers, 87 Union Street
(08456) 015 929

Ideal for transport around the city as it covers a wider area than the underground and isn't affected by traffic congestion. Ticket prices start at around £1.45.

National Rail Enquiries
(08457) 484 950

Got an enquiry about trains? Then you'll be wanting to call the helpful chaps over at National Rail Enquiries. NB This does not apply to train anoraks who want to ask questions about the gauge of track size, engine types, or model numbers. There are helplines for you people.

PLANES

BAA Glasgow Airport
Paisley, Renfrewshire
(08700) 400 008

For both international and domestic flights. Call or go online for general enquires. Visit www.firstgroup.com for info on train/bus express routes to the airport.

Glasgow Tourist Information Centre
11 George Square
(0141) 204 4400

The centre focuses on accommodation, although the website does provide a link to a message board where other tourists can offer advice. Located slap-bang in the city centre, just where it should be.

Useful info

BURGER

McDonalds
209 Argyle Street
(0141) 572 1770

We don't care that corporate America has taken over, because it tastes so damn good.

🕐 *Mon–Thu & Sun, 6am–11pm; Fri–Sat, 6am–12am*
🍴 *Double cheeseburger, 99p*

CHICKEN

KFC
178 Argyle Street
(0141) 248 8361

They do chicken. What they call chicken.

🕐 *Mon–Sat, 10.30am–11pm; Sun, 12pm–11pm*
🍴 *Sweetcorn, £1*

FISH & CHIPS

Mr Chips
476 Sauchiehall Street
(0141) 332 6226

Does what it says on the tin. Great chips.

🕐 *Mon–Wed, 7pm–12.30am; Thu–Sun, 7pm–4.00am*
🍴 *Single sausage, £2.30*

SANDWICHES

Subway
249 West George Street
(0141) 305 5322

🕐 *Mon–Wed, 9am–10pm; Thu–Sat, 9pm–1am; Sun, 11am–10pm*
🍴 *6-inch meatball (with a drink and a cookie or crisps), £3.99*

PIZZA

Domino's Pizza
530 Great Western Road
(0141) 337 3379

Bog-standard pizzas for lazy arses.

🕐 *Mon–Thu, 12pm–11.30pm; Fri–Sun, 12pm–12am*
🍴 *Cheese steak melt (large), £12.99*

Little Italy
205 Byres Road
(0141) 330 6287

The tiny tables are perfect for the primary class who clearly made the Last Supper model that's on the wall. With their elbows.

🕐 *Mon–Thu, 8am–10pm; Fri & Sat, 8am–1am; Sun, 5pm–10pm*
🍴 *Pizza meatball and green peppers, £5*

ORIENTAL

Canton Express
407 Sauchiehall Street
(0141) 332 0145

Tastes fantastic, but after 33 vodkas and coke, so would kitchen utensils.

🕐 *Mon–Sun, 12pm–4am*
🍴 *Anything, £5.50*

Glasgow Noodle Bar
488 Sauchiehall Street
(0141) 333 1883

For a noodle bar they're not the best at noodles. They even get their watery soup wrong. It tastes like something out of a homeless lady's shopping bag.

🕐 *Mon–Sun, 9am–5am*
🍴 *Chicken and sweetcorn soup, £2*

SAFETY

Police
Glasgow Police Department, 201 South Broadway
(0141) 651 5151

Accident and emergency
Glasgow Royal Infirmary, 84 Castle Street
(0141) 211 4000

Doctor
Rochdale Place Surgery, 10 Rochdale Place
(0141) 776 2468

NHS Dentist
Glasgow Dental Hospital, 378 Sauchiehall Street
(0141) 211 9600

Family planning
The Sandyford Initiative, 2 Sandyford Place
(0141) 211 8130

Rape Helpline
(0141) 552 3201

Samaritans
(0141) 248 4488
Providing confidential, emotional support 24 hours a day.

Fire and rescue service
Glasgow Fire Department, 203 South Broadway
(0141) 651 5170

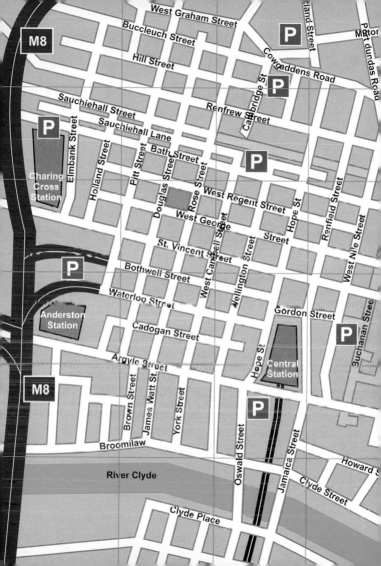

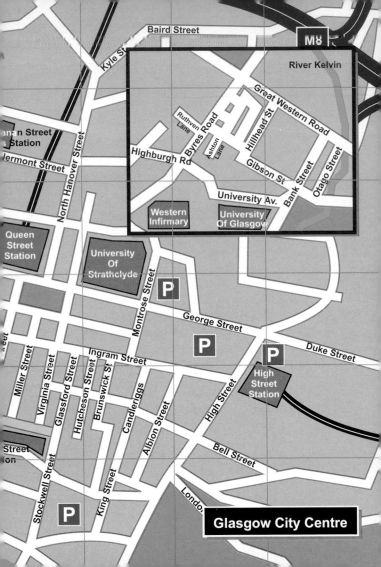

Glasgow City Centre

Itchy

CALLING ALL ASPIRING SCRIBBLERS...

We need cheeky writers to contribute their sparkling talents to the next issue of the Itchy City magazine.

We want the inside track on the bars, pubs, clubs and restaurants in your city, as well as longer features and dynamic pictures to represent the comedy, art, music, theatre, cinema and sport scenes in your city.

If you're interested in getting involved, please send examples of your writing to: editor@itchymedia.co.uk, clearly stating which city you can work in. All work will be fully credited.

Bath/Birmingham/Brighton/Bristol/Cardiff/Edinburgh/Glasgow/
Leeds/Liverpool/London/Manchester/Nottingham/
Oxford/Sheffield/York

Index